JESUS
AMONG
OTHER
GODS

JESUS AMONG OTHER GODS

YOUTH EDITION

Ravi Zacharias
and
Kevin Johnson

WORD PUBLISHING

NASHVILLE

A Thomas Nelson Company

Published by Word Publishing, a unit of Thomas Nelson, Inc., P.O. Box 141000, Nashville, Tennessee 37214. No portion of this book may be reproduced, stored in a retrieval system, or transmitted in any form or by any means—electronic, mechanical, photocopy, recording, or other—except for brief quotations in printed reviews, without the prior permission of the publisher.

Scripture quotations used in this book are from the Holy Bible, New International Version, copyright © 1973, 1978, 1984, International Bible Society. Used by permission of Zondervan Bible Publishers.

ISBN 0-8499-4217-9

Printed in the United States of America

00 01 02 03 04 05 PHX 9 8 7 6 5 4 3 2 1

CONTENTS

ONE

MEETING MY MASTER

How was school?" my father asked.

He had never asked me that before. My report card always gave him more than enough information to jump-start an argument. I should have known there was something behind his sudden curiosity, but without any suspicion I answered, "Fine."

I was a sixteen-year-old student in a community college, taking advantage of a shortcut to finishing high school. Each day at the time classes normally ended, I cycled home. From my point of view, my day had been like any other. But this one was going to end differently.

Normally my father wouldn't have been home at that time of day, but there he was, standing with his arms stretched across the open doorway as if to block me out of the house. I glanced at him. His eyes burned back at me.

My charade was over.

I hadn't been at school that day.

In fact, I hadn't been at school for a lot of days.

I had spent month after month wandering the streets on my bike looking for a sports match I could watch or maybe even play in. After cutting all my classes, I would show up for tests and squeak through.

I won't repeat my father's exact language, but the rage he unleashed on me and the thrashing he gave me left me trembling and sobbing. If my mother hadn't stepped in, I could have been seriously hurt.

Getting Inside My Head

This is a book about the absolute truth of Jesus—how He stands in a class by Himself, how in a world that believes in many gods He is the one true God. But I want you to know some of my story, because it has everything to do with how I came to believe Jesus is who He said He is: the answer to our deepest longings and the only way to God. I want to share with you

the *true belief*

in a *true person*

who gave me *true help*.

This run-in with my father brought me to a screeching halt. It forced me to ask myself some hard questions. Why was I skipping classes? You might think I just hated school—that I was infected with a bad case of senioritis that arrived several semesters ahead of schedule. You might even think I was ingenious or courageous or devious to do what many students only wish they could do.

But my motivation to skip school ran much deeper than that. Even though no one who knew me would have suspected how I felt, I struggled with emptiness on the inside. I had questions. I thought life made no sense, but I didn't know where to turn for answers. I didn't know if answers even existed. I wondered if everyone else was as confused as I was but better able to mask it. I worried I was one of an unlucky few who simply thought too much.

A World of Pressure

I grew up in India. While to you that may seem a world away, the pressures I faced were very similar to those you face. My father was highly successful and influential, and if I didn't succeed, I was nothing.

My dad was determined to find a brilliant career for me.

I was just as determined to live for sports—a love of my life in which he had no interest.

He had a point. Every boy I knew wanted to grow up to play cricket for India, just as every kid in New York wants to play baseball for the Yankees. But I did have some talent. At my college I managed to play for many teams—cricket, hockey, tennis, and table tennis—yet never once did my dad come to see me play, even in any big game.

Probably the most wrenching words I ever heard my father say to me were, "You will never make anything of your life!" And honestly, it seemed he was right.

The ache I felt on the inside was intensified by pressure on the outside. It started with school itself. Competition was everything. Each of us was defined by our success or failure in school. It wasn't enough merely to do well; we had to be at the top of our class. When I was in school, every student's grades and class rank were printed in the newspapers for all to see. Success or failure marked us for public pride or shame. One of my closest friends toyed with suicide after his high-school finals because he didn't rank first in the entire city of New Delhi, the capital of India. Another one of my classmates in college actually burned himself to death because he didn't make the grade.

> One of my classmates in college burned himself to death because he didn't make the grade.

3

A lifetime of pressure awaited after high school. The pressure to look good and perform well was everywhere. Every day in my homeland, in fact—this is maybe worse than having your picture on the back of a milk carton—hundreds of advertisements are printed in the "matrimonial" section of newspapers by parents looking for spouses for their children. Every prospective bride and groom is advertised as being from "a good home" and searching for someone from "a good home." "My son graduated first in his class." "My daughter won a scholarship to study in England." "My son is an engineer." "My daughter is a doctor." Those were the dreams—my father's dreams—to which I was to aspire.

Can you sense something of the weight I felt? Maybe you feel something like that too—many expectations of others piled on top of many doubts in your own mind about whether you have what it takes to make it in life. I flirted with failure in numerous directions, and you can imagine how I upset my father.

Finding God: 330-Million-to-One

The night of my thrashing I stood punished and facing a wall. I wished my father and I could talk, but we didn't have that type of relationship—and you can't create heart-to-heart communication in an instant. (Years later, by the way, we did talk. My father became a Christian later in life, and he was extremely proud of the path I took in ministry. We eventually built the relationship we never figured out when I was young.)

The pressure of the situation ultimately led me to my heavenly Father. That night I began my intense search for answers that led me to Jesus Christ.

I want you to understand that my trusting Christ happened in a culture that is overwhelmingly Hindu. That in itself is a miracle. Though some in my family had been Christians, on both my mother's and my father's side, my family had not long before come from the highest caste of the Hindu priesthood. India is a land full of gods—330 *million* gods, to be exact. Searching for the one true God in that environment is almost laughable. I would say that the odds were 330-million-to-one that I should have found spiritual satisfaction in something other than Christianity. But I was hungry for *reality*. And *reality* is only found in Jesus.

A Supermarket of Religions

So in that supermarket of gods, how could I push past aisle after aisle of Eastern religions to hunt down and pack my cart full of Christian truth?

You might hear people talk about the "myth of Christian uniqueness," that Christianity is no better, no more believable, or no more beneficial than any other religion. What's more, some argue that spreading faith is wrong and that converting from one religion to another should be banned. Some think it's wrong for me to tell you the "right" way to believe and live. But I came to Christ because I am convinced of the absolute truth of His message—not just that what I believe *sounds nice* or even that it *works,* but that it is *real*.

Back to that spiritual supermarket. When I reached out my hand to choose my faith, I wanted something so true that its reality would fill me up. I wasn't looking for a small, cheap, microwaveable meal in which all the flavors run together. The last thing I wanted was to be fooled by an empty carton—pretty on the outside, nothing on the inside. I was hungry for reality. And I recognized Jesus was real.

But Aren't All Religions the Same?

If you have been raised in the church, you probably believe that the Christian faith is the real thing, true beyond any doubt. Have you noticed how many people, though, don't share your faith? People all around you could chime in with the words I heard a thousand times growing up in India: "We all come through different routes and end up in the same place"; in other words, we all follow different faiths, but they all lead us to the same God.

American culture is rapidly adopting this stance toward non-Christian religions. Our society is becoming more and more "pluralistic," accepting all religions not only as alternative options but as equally correct views of life. Anything you believe sincerely enough, religious pluralists say, will get you to God—and to heaven. You might hear it said like this:

"It doesn't matter what you believe—just that you believe it strongly."

"Every faith leads to God."

"All religions teach the same things."

When you hear a teacher or a friend or your favorite movie star making those claims, nodding your head in agreement seems polite. That's pluralism in action. On the surface, pluralism makes everyone feel warmly accepted. But it doesn't get us to the real facts of life.

Hang On Tight to Truth

If you tell a friend that you are a dachshund, you will be laughed at—or locked up. But if you say you *worship* that same wiener dog, pluralists tell us to celebrate your sincere belief and to accept it as true—just as true as the well-substantiated evidence for Christianity. In the first case, most people would probably say, "We can see with our own eyes that you aren't a dachshund." In the second case, people increasingly say, "I support your belief. I respect your sincere worship of wiener dogs."

Have you noticed how some people will applaud just about any spiritual idea—up to and including the divinity of wiener dogs—but bristle if you try to take a stand that any spiritual idea is *absolutely* true? That a certain behavior is *always* wrong? Or that your Christian faith is a truth that should be accepted by *everyone?* Again, that's pluralism in action.

Can You Really Find Answers to Religious Questions?

You want the surgeon who operates on your brain to know the facts of physiology. You know to supply the correct answers on your history exam—or you will fail. You can add two plus two and get four in any universe. But isn't religion different? Are the answers we can find really that sure?

We wouldn't have sure answers—except for one thing. The beliefs of Christianity aren't pulled from thin air. The strongest evidences for the Christian faith are the things Jesus said and did when He came to live on earth. Because of that, we can prove beyond any reasonable doubt His existence. We can read His words with certainty of their accuracy. And our minds can examine the hard facts of history surrounding His resurrection. The sure answers of your Christian faith are rooted in tough-to-dispute facts.

Society's rules aren't hard to figure out:

- *Philosophically,* you can believe anything, so long as you don't claim it's true.

- *Morally,* you can practice anything, so long as you don't claim it's a better way.

- *Religiously,* you can hold to anything, so long as you don't mention Jesus Christ.

> **All religions are *not* the same. All religions do *not* point to God. All religions do *not* say that all religions are the same.**

We live in a time when nerves are at the surface, easily set on edge. It's easy to offend or to get into heated arguments. That isn't my goal. But in our real-life struggles between right and wrong, justice and injustice, life and death, we all realize that truth does matter. Real answers count for everything. If you and I are going to deal in reality, what matters most isn't *sincerity* but *truth.* I want beliefs that correspond to what is objectively true.

The Truth About Religions

It's a catastrophic mistake to think that all religions are right and that it doesn't matter whether their claims are actually true or not. I have spent my life studying the absolute truth of the Christian message, especially as it relates to other religious teachings. I can say with confidence several things:

- All religions are *not* the same.
- All religions do *not* point to God.
- All religions do *not* say that all religions are the same.

- At the heart of *every* religion is a stubborn commitment to a particular way of defining who God is or isn't—and a particular way of defining life's purpose.

I say these things confidently because I can demonstrate my claims. People who say that all religions are the same not only show their ignorance of all religions, but they also hold a warped view of even the best-known ones. Every religion at its core is exclusive—in other words, every religion requires people to follow what it says is true and right.

The Intolerance Test

I frequently hear people say Christianity is intolerant. After all, it calls all people—no exceptions—to think and to act as God commands. It requires all people to bow to Jesus alone. Yet in that sense, all religions are intolerant. Every religion requires people to follow what it says is true and right.

"Believe like I do" is easy to spot as an intolerant or "exclusive" claim. But other statements sound more accepting, like "You have to let people believe what they want." But you can put the plea for openness to this test: Ask yourself, "What does the person mean by 'You must be open to everything'?" What it almost always means is, "You must be open to everything that I am open to and disagree with anything I disagree with."

The person who sounds tolerant will never leave you free to believe as you wish. That's intolerance—and the worst kind of intolerance, because it is intolerance that doesn't admit it is being intolerant!

An Honest Look at Other Faiths

I worry about Christian young people who don't understand the reliability of Christianity's claims to truthfulness. I also worry they are being drawn to false religions made to look real and attractive.

In today's culture, if a spiritual idea is Eastern—from a place like India or China—it is off-limits to criticism. If an idea is Western—judged to be from mainstream European or North American culture—it's open season for insults. A journalist can walk into a church and mock its services, but he or she dare not find fault in a Buddhist or Hindu or Islamic ceremony.

There is a whole mass of non-Christian beliefs—sometimes bizarre—you won't hear criticized, whether in textbooks or on TV. Two examples:

- While I was writing this book, I attended several Eastern festivals of worship. At one of these, followers had huge numbers of hooks inserted into their bodies. Assistants pulled on thongs tied to the hooks to exert pressure on the skin. Knives were pierced through their faces and small spears through their tongues. It's a terrifying sight. I have to wonder why teachers and philosophers who criticize Christianity don't also condemn these Eastern practices.

- Closer to home, you can walk into any non-Christian bookstore and see the writings of Deepak Chopra. He teaches a brand of spirituality, success, and prosperity woven with Vedic teachings (teachings from Hindu scriptures), karma (the Eastern belief that you always get what you have coming), and self-deification (the mystical teaching that you are god). But millions who follow those ideas live in mind-numbing poverty. What's wrong with this picture?

Our job isn't to endlessly criticize the beliefs of others. But it *is* our task to sort truth from falsehood—and to understand why our own faith is true.

The One-of-a-Kind Jesus

The goal of *Jesus Among Other Gods* is to demonstrate how you can know Jesus Christ is who He claimed to be—the Son of the Living God, the One who came to seek and to save a world of people who are far from Him. You are living in a time when the West is looking more like the East, and the East is quietly imitating the West. Religions like Hinduism and Buddhism are making a revival, but often as a mix of slick Western media and Eastern mythology—a deadly and seductive combination. The first casualty of these alternative blends of spirituality is truth— and when we lose truth, we lose God.

It's incredibly easy to be sold on Eastern spirituality, for example, when we find out that our favorite Hollywood movie star practices Buddhism. We succumb to a personality and swallow the idea, say, that it's possible to be good without having God—all without thinking through the belief system and seeing the emptiness of the ideas. I want to teach you to *think* through your faith so you can grapple with a belief system without giving up on the people you hold dear.

Please understand that the belief that the facts of Christianity add up to something absolutely, always, no-doubt-about-it *true*— while the teachings of other religions do not—didn't start with me. Jesus never accepted all religious systems as equal in terms of truth.

Jesus, in fact, dared to say some highly exclusive things about Himself—things that leave us no choice but to agree or disagree. If these things are true, they make other religions false. Jesus said to the apostle Thomas, for example, that "I am the way and the truth and the life. No one comes to the Father except through me" (John 14:6).

Just look at the claims contained in that statement:

- First and foremost, Jesus asserted *there is only one way to God.* That shocks many people. And it disagrees with the teachings of Hinduism and Bahaism, which have long challenged the concept of a single way to God.

- Jesus stated without a doubt that *God is the author of life* and that *meaning in life is found in knowing Him.* This idea would be totally denied by Buddhism, which either ignores God or rules out His existence altogether.

- Jesus revealed that *He was the Son of God who led the way to the Father.* Islam considers that claim damnably wrong. How could God have a son?

- Jesus claimed that *we can personally know God* and the absolute nature of His truth. Agnostics say we can't be sure who God is.

Every word of Jesus' statement challenges the basic spiritual beliefs of many of the people around you. And it clashed completely with the Indian culture from which I came. But this is what we have to answer: Was Jesus *right?* Are His claims *true?*

I believe there is overwhelming evidence to support all of Jesus' claims. We can study the life of Christ and show that He was and is the way, the truth, and the life. Each chapter of this book, in fact, will give you a different angle on Jesus. We will look at six questions or challenges put to Jesus—and how His answers are unique and uniquely believable among the world's religions.

- In chapter 2, we see how the first disciples of Jesus insisted on asking Jesus, "Where do You live?" They were asking, *Who are You?*

- In chapter 3, we hear the enemies of Jesus challenging Him with "What miraculous sign can You give us so we will believe?" They wanted to know, *How do we know You are who You claim to be?*

- In chapter 4, the crowds tell Jesus that "Our fathers ate manna in the desert. . . . Why don't You give us the same?" They wondered, *Aren't You going to make life wonderful for us?*

- In chapter 5, we hear people asking, "Is God the source of suffering?" They needed to know, *Is God kind—or cruel?*

- In chapter 6, the opponents of Jesus ask, "Aren't You going to answer?" They wondered, *Aren't You going to answer every last question we ask?*

We can't look at every religion in this book, so we will focus on the three major belief systems mentioned briefly so far: Hinduism, Buddhism, and Islam. We will also hear from atheism—a belief system built on the denial of God's existence. And to finish, in chapter 7, we see one final question asked by an angel on Jesus' behalf: "Who are you looking for?" or, *What kind of God do you want?*

A Bit More of My Story . . .

You probably figured out that my fight with my father hadn't given me answers, only more questions. One day soon after the fight, my sister was invited to a youth event. She invited me to attend with her, and the visiting speaker turned out to be an internationally respected Christian leader. My memory of the meeting is blurry, but this much I know: He spoke on the best-known verse in the Bible, "For God so loved the world that he gave his one and only Son, that whoever believes in him shall not perish but have eternal life" (John 3:16).

I was pulled not only by the speaker's words but also by his heart. At his invitation to trust in Jesus Christ as my Lord and my Savior, I responded by walking awkwardly to the front— alone. I didn't really understand what I was doing. Although I had been raised in a church, I had so little idea that its message had anything to do with life that I grasped only part of what he said. Yet I knew that my life was wrong and that I needed some-body to make it right. I wanted new hungers, new longings, new directions, and new loves. I knew God had to matter. I just didn't know how to find Him.

Isn't This Supposed to Get Easier?

I left that night with a hint in my mind that something about the message was totally right, even though I hadn't put it all together. As weeks went by, I continued to attend all of the pop-ular Hindu festivals and to enjoy watching dramatic presenta-tions of their mythology. I had a committed Hindu friend who tried hard to get me to embrace the Hindu view of life.

Then a very significant event took place. I was cycling past a cre-mation site and stopped to ask a Hindu priest where that person— whose body was nothing more than a pile of ashes—was now.

"Young man," he said, "that is a question you will be asking all your life, and you will never find a certain answer."

If that's the best a priest can do, I thought, *what hope is there for a spiritual beginner like me?*

Months went by. Without Christian teaching to build on what

How Do You Spot Spiritual Hunger?

You might think, Ravi, I don't have the huge doubts you had. Am I less spiritual? I know that every person in the world doesn't ask exactly the questions I did or struggle in the same way. But I also know that all human beings—you and your friends included—are spiritually hungry. Do you doubt me? Try this:

1. Look outward. You can't deny the fact that people are incurably religious. You can see it in sheer numbers, like the three-quarters of a billion people in India who are Hindu. You can read it in poetry and racks of magazines and best-selling books. You can hear it in chart-topping songs. You even hear hunger in the voices of people who push God away. The famous atheist Madelyn Murray O'Hair once said, "I wish someone would love me." That's a spiritual hunger.

2. Look inward. It was on the night that NFL superstar Deion Sanders won the Super Bowl that he realized his spiritual hunger. To celebrate his world championship, he climbed into bed and ordered a Lamborghini sports car, but he still felt empty. All the winning wasn't enough to fill him up. Have you felt that too—that only God is big enough? That's a spiritual hunger.

I had experienced, I was haunted by the same doubts about the purpose of life. I hadn't solved any of my conflicts with my father or answered any of my questions. And it led to a tragic moment.

> I found myself on a hospital bed, having been rushed there after an attempted suicide.

I made a firm but calm decision. A quiet exit would save my family and me any further failure. I put my plan into action. As a result, I found myself on a hospital bed, having been rushed there after an attempted suicide.

From the Brink

In that hospital room, someone brought me a Bible and read me a passage of Scripture. I could still hear the speaker's message from that youth event, and it gave me a base on which to build. He had taught from John 3—about God's love. Now I was hearing from John 14—about God's purpose.

Jesus spoke the words in John 14 to the apostle Thomas, who later took Jesus' claims to India and paid for that message with his life. Thomas's memorial is just a few miles from where I was born. Jesus said to him, "I am the way and the truth and the life. No one comes to the Father except through me" (v. 6). But what captured my attention at that moment were words further along, when Jesus said to His disciples, "Because I live, you also will live."

Again, I wasn't sure what all that meant. I pieced together God's love in Christ, the way that was provided because of Christ, and the promise of life through Him—and on that hospital bed I made my commitment to put my life in His hands. I turned my life completely over to Jesus Christ.

Why I Came to Jesus and Why I Stay

When I was able to leave the hospital, I was a new person. No, I didn't have everything figured out. But Christ was part of my life, and the change was more dramatic than I could have ever imagined.

The Jesus I know and love today I met at the age of seventeen. Here's the best part: His character and His tug in my life mean infinitely more now than they did when I first surrendered my life to Him.

1. I came to Him because I didn't know which way to turn. I stick with Him because there is no other way I want to turn.

2. I came to Him aching for something I didn't have. I stick with Him because I have something I won't trade.

Why Can't You Live Without Purpose?

You might think I'm just uptight—wanting to know truth, trying hard to find a purpose bigger than a bat and ball. Maybe I sound just like your parents.

Here's why you can't live without the undergirding purpose of having God in your life: You can't run from reality. Your questions don't go away. Whatever hurts or dissatisfactions you feel only fester. And the more you run from truth, the more you realize you can't escape it.

And if the ultimate truth in the universe is that God exists, that He came in the person of Jesus Christ, and that He wants to have a relationship with you—then that's a reality you will want to hang on to tightly.

JESUS AMONG OTHER GODS

3. I came to Him as a stranger. I stick with Him as a close friend.

4. I came to Him unsure about my future. I stick with Him sure about my eternal destiny.

5. I came to Him from a culture with 330 million gods. I stick with Him knowing that He alone is God.

What strikes me now is that I not only found truth to answer my questions, but I also found meaning to meet my discouragement. God didn't just teach me about Himself. He pulled me close to Himself. He gave me not just a correct way to think but also a reason to live.

The God Who Gives You Purpose

Life needs purpose like a body needs a skeleton, yet my pursuits had no supporting structure. I drifted through sports and relationships, but I had no ultimate purpose. Just think of the alternatives our culture gives to us as reasons to live—pleasure, wealth, power, fame, fate, charity, peace, education, pride in the country or neighborhood where we are born—the list is endless. None of those, though, is a match for knowing Jesus.

Purpose is what God wants to give you too. God is no abstract idea. He is the infinite, yet personal King of the Universe. Knowing the truth about God means you can truly know Him and live the life He plans for you.

I moved to Canada with my family when I was twenty. I have found that many young people here understand their desperate need for purpose better than adults. Why? Adults can be cynical. They think they know what works and what doesn't. Young people are like new millionaires—they invest their hearts in one thing or another, and they are figuring out what pays off. But their pleasures and frustrations are fresh, and they aren't afraid to talk about their needs. They are also more open to discovering how God will meet those needs.

Weaving Your Life

I can't know every question of your mind or hurt of your heart. But I do know that a purposeful design emerges when God weaves a pattern from what might seem to us like a mess of a life.

I once visited a place where beautiful saris are made. The sari is the long, flowing garment worn by Indian women, usually about six yards of fabric. Wedding saris are a work of art—rich in gold and silver threads, dazzling with colors.

The place I was visiting was said to make the best wedding saris in the world. I expected to see elaborate machines spinning mind-boggling designs. I was wrong! Each sari was made individually by a father-and-son team. The father sat above on a platform two to three feet higher than the son, surrounded by several spools of thread—some dark, some shining. The son did just one thing. At a nod from his father, he would move a guide from one side to the other and back again. The father would gather some threads in his fingers, nod once more, and the son would move the guide again. This would be repeated for hundreds of hours, until a magnificent pattern emerged.

The son had the easy task—just to move at the father's nod. All along, the father had the design in his mind. It was his job to bring the right threads together.

The more I reflect on my own life and look at the lives of others, I am fascinated to see the design God has for each one of us if we just respond to His nods.

But to respond to God's nods you have to trust Him. And to trust Him you need to be sure of your answer to this question: Is Jesus who He claimed to be?

TWO

WHERE DO YOU LIVE?

I was barely a teenager when my seven-year-old brother had the rare privilege of meeting the queen of England. At that time, Queen Elizabeth was the ceremonial leader not only of one of the most powerful nations on earth but of an empire that still spanned much of the globe. My brother, as the youngest member of the choir at the Delhi Cathedral, was to be formally introduced to the queen following a Sunday church service. Unknown to us, his meeting with the queen was televised on the news back in England. A swarm of viewers called the station to ask whether "that cute little boy" was available for adoption. Ever since that day, we have had a line ready whenever he acted up. "Maybe," we would say, "we should have taken the English up on their offer!"

Meeting the queen had all the stress and excitement of meeting any famous person, and then some. We piled advice on my brother to prepare him for his extraordinary meeting—the right way to bow, to stand, and to speak with utmost respect. We repeatedly coached him to address the queen as "Your Majesty" and not as "Auntie," a typical way of showing respect in India. He was, when the moment came, a raging success.

Meeting historic figures is no ordinary experience. The

grander the event, the greater your fear of goofing up. So you rehearse your lines. You debate what to ask. And you wonder: *What if I freeze? What if I miss my once-in-a-lifetime moment?*

Flashback Two Thousand Years

I can only imagine the talk at Andrew and Simon Peter's home when they first met Jesus. Andrew confidently told their family they had met Israel's Savior, the only hope for a nation trapped by a series of cruel foreign rulers. Back in Bible times, any good Israelite had prayed for the coming of the One the Bible prophesied would free His people.

At supper, a cynical family member probably choked on his food when Andrew announced that he had just met the long-awaited deliverer. Andrew and Simon Peter no doubt needed to protest over and over that they weren't out of their minds. They had talked to Jesus. They had spent hours with Him. Andrew had even had the chance to ask Him whatever he wished.

Out of sheer curiosity, someone at the table surely said, "So what exactly did you ask Him?"

"I asked Him," came Andrew's confident reply, "where He lived" (John 1:38).

Didn't You Think to Ask . . . ?

The Bible doesn't describe what happened at home. But can't you imagine the silence around the table? Andrew had been in the presence of someone he believed to be the greatest being ever to walk the planet. And all he asked was, "Where do You live?"

If you don't want to mess up when you meet a monarch, think how much more you would want to speak wisely when you met your Master, the Messiah.

"That was the best you could do, Andrew? To ask Him *where*

He lived? What did you expect Him to say? 'Nazareth. Fourth house past the Rent-a-Donkey stand'?"

Is that all Andrew wanted? A street address?

Suppose you were able to ask Jesus one question. What would *you* ask?

You can probably think of better questions to put Jesus to the test. Andrew could have talked politics: "What do you think of the Roman government's practice of hanging people on crosses?"

What Would You Ask Jesus?

Suppose you had an hour to interview Jesus Himself—a face-to-face, journalistic meeting. Take a few minutes to think what you would ask. What deep questions do you hear other people wondering about God?

It's intriguing how silent the Scriptures are on many issues. What kind of home did Jesus live in? What kind of work did He do? How much did He earn? What did He wear? What did He look like? Did His mother do His laundry? How was His home furnished?

It wouldn't have been that hard to preserve a couch or a piece of clothing for us to put in a museum for the world to see. In Turkey, we can see the sword of Mohammed and strands of hair claimed to have come from his beard. Recently, someone reported finding a tooth of Gautama, the Buddha.

So why is Scripture silent on these run-of-the-mill details? To His followers, what Jesus wore must have seemed trivial compared to who He was. And, as we will see, His earthly roots weren't as crucial as His heavenly home.

Or, "Do you have any comment on the fact that Caesar thinks he is divine?" Or he could have asked Jesus deep, spiritual questions: "John the Baptizer—that locust-eating desert dweller—says you are the 'Lamb of God'? What does he mean? Are you headed for a gruesome end?" Or Andrew simply could have asked, "For nearly two thousand years the prophets have told us of the Savior's coming. Are you truly the Christ, the Anointed One? Could You give me half a dozen reasons why I should believe in You?"

In that serious encounter, I doubt any of us would have asked what Andrew did. Yet I'm convinced his question was truly wise, the start of his serious investigation of Jesus. The answer to that astounding question—"Where do You live?"—would tell Andrew all about Jesus' beginnings. And Jesus' answer demonstrates to *us* how absolutely different Jesus is from all other religious heroes.

Where Did You Say You're From?

You have probably guessed from what I have shared about my growing up that in the East—whether in India or Israel—home is a potent place. In fact, it determines who you are. It assigns your rank in the social order. It tells the whole world whether your future looks bright or dim. Figure out someone's home, and you find out absolutely everything.

Actually, what Andrew wanted to know isn't all that different from crucial information you want when you meet a stranger. Adults ask, "So where do you work?" or "What do you do?" Youth are quick with "So what school do you go to?" and "What do your parents do?" Fairly or unfairly, from those answers you form a picture—everything from family income and social status to intelligence and personality. You might even pop Andrew's all-encompassing question, "So where do You live?"

Where I grew up, the big questions are exactly what Andrew

asked. "What was your home city?" "Which part of town did you live in?" In a hierarchical society—one in which a person's place in the social ladder is clearly assigned—your home address gives the inquirer a wealth of information about you.

My point is that with that one question, Andrew is trying to peg Jesus—not in order to be rude or disrespectful, but to figure Him out.

Wouldn't You Like to Know?

Jesus' answer builds the intrigue. He didn't offer a zip code or a street name. He simply said, "Come and see." The would-be disciples went with Him to see where He was staying and evidently spent the night there (John 1:39). Andrew returned to tell his brother Simon that they had found the Messiah—the Christ—and invited him to meet Jesus too (vv. 40–42).

The next day another soon-to-be follower was told to "come and see." Philip, who was from the same city as Andrew and Simon Peter, invited Nathanael

> Suppose you could interview Jesus face-to-face. What would you ask Him?

to join them. Philip's pitch was strong: "We have found the one Moses wrote about in the Law, and about whom the prophets also wrote—Jesus of Nazareth, the son of Joseph" (vv. 43–45). There you have it—the all-important information about home city and parents.

Nathanael wasn't impressed. He reacted the way you might upon hearing that your rival high school or the backwoods town you joke about had produced a sports star or a Hollywood celebrity. "Nazareth!" he smirked. "Can anything good come from there?" (v. 46). Philip gave him the same challenge to see Jesus for himself.

Nathanael met far more than he expected. While Jesus knew that Nathanael didn't think very much of His hometown, He also knew Nathanael was a genuine seeker of truth—when they met, Jesus called him "a true Israelite, in whom there is nothing false." And then Jesus told him He had seen him before Philip called him, sitting under a fig tree (vv. 47–48).

We have no idea what Nathanael was pondering under the fig tree. But Nathanael reacted with startled awe to Jesus' supernatural knowledge of his character and location: "Rabbi, you are the Son of God," he declared. "You are the King of Israel" (v. 49).

Jesus' Real Address

Andrew thought the best way to uncover whether Jesus was who He said He was would be to follow Him to His house—to the earthly address of the One who claimed to be the Son of God. But Jesus Himself had much more to reveal than any home could show. Andrew was asking, "Jesus, where are You from?" And Jesus, by His words and actions, declared this in response:

- *I'm not merely from this earth.* Nathanael asked, "Can anything good come out of Nazareth?" A few verses later we hear, "Is this not the son of Joseph, the carpenter?" The people around Jesus were puzzled that the Messiah could come from a family of such modest professional status, not to mention such a backward city. Nazareth was hardly on the map. It took biblical archaeologists years even to pinpoint Nazareth.

  Jesus took their attention in a new direction. It's as if Jesus is saying, "Andrew, you want to know where I am from? You have no idea! The only way you can understand Me is if you come and get to know Me." They were in for a shock—and in need of a long explanation. Jesus would never be merely their new friend, the son of a carpenter from Nazareth. He was infinitely more. As important as His earthly parentage was, His home address wasn't an earthly one—because He had no beginning.

- *I came from heaven.* Andrew, Simon Peter, Philip, and Nathanael all were wrapped up in where Jesus lived. Jesus was about to unveil where He was truly from. He said, "You believe because I told you I saw you under the fig tree. You shall see greater things than that. . . . I tell you the truth, you shall see heaven open, and the angels of God ascending and descending on the Son of Man" (v. 50).

Not only did Jesus have supernatural knowledge of Nathanael that only God could possess (as in Ps. 139:1–10), but He also spoke of Himself in a picture that pointed back to how God revealed

> To ask for the "where" of Jesus' home is the same as asking the "when" of God's beginning.

Himself in the Old Testament (Gen. 28:12). Later, Jesus said specifically that He came "from above" (John 3:31; 8:23).

The new disciples concluded that Jesus had come from His heavenly Father, the God of their heroes Abraham, Isaac, and Jacob. They were right. The words of Jesus about a heavenly dwelling and angels ascending and descending to serve Him point to the fact that He is the Lord of heaven and earth. He had existed eternally. He had no beginning. To ask for the "where" of Jesus' home is the same as asking the "when" of God's beginning. He had come from a place they could hardly fathom. Jesus, in short, said, "Are you shocked because I told you about yourself? Wait until you fully see who I am and grasp where I am truly from!"

Truth Tip: Who Is the God of the Bible?

When Jesus said "I and the Father are one" (John 10:30), He claimed to possess God's being, power, and moral attributes. The New Testament writer Paul expressed the same thought this way: "In Christ all the fullness of the Deity lives in bodily form" (Col. 2:9). Take a look through the Bible to see exactly how great God is:

- Genesis says that He is the Creator of all that exists (Gen. 1:1–2:2).

- Exodus declares that He is holy and will tolerate no rivals (Exod. 20:1–17).

- Kings and Chronicles display His in-depth involvement in human history (2 Chron. 16:9).

- Psalms shows He is a God who loves music and art (Ps.100).

- Proverbs displays His wisdom for everyday life (Prov. 2).

- Isaiah says no god we could invent can compare to Him (Isa. 40).

- Jeremiah unveils God's compassion for His suffering people (Lam. 3).

- Hosea demonstrates God's love even for followers who fail (Hos. 2:14–3:3).

- Daniel illustrates how God can be trusted to take care of His own (Dan. 6).

- Malachi points out that God wants pure worshipers (Mal.1–4).

- The Gospels prove God lived as one of us so we can know He understands us (Matt.–John; Heb.4:15–16).

- Revelation gives a glimpse of God's dazzling glory (Rev. 4).

- *I am God—the Father and I are one.* Jesus was just beginning to reveal His true identity. His followers had obtained just a glimpse. John, the disciple and Bible writer who told their story, offers this full-blown explanation of who Jesus was: "In the beginning was the Word, and the Word was *with* God, and the Word *was* God" (John 1:1; emphasis added). It's a clear echo of the start of the Bible: "In the beginning God . . ." (Gen. 1:1).

So Jesus claimed to be God. But is it true? How can we be sure? Where is He really from? Nathanael met Jesus and arrived at an instant conclusion: "Jesus, You are the Son of God." But how can *we* be sure?

Prove It to Me, Part 1: The Virgin Birth

A skeptic might ask, "Well, Jesus might claim to be from heaven, but how do we know where He really came from?" The Bible offers two convincing facts:

- He had unique origins—born to a virgin
- He had unique character—pure beyond compare

Unlike any other religious leader in history, Jesus had an origin that hinted at His real, eternal origin. And unlike any other religious leader in history, Jesus displayed a perfectly flawless, perfectly trustworthy character.

When you were younger, your parents may have told you fantastic tales about where you came from. One couple I know wanted to avoid telling their children the story of the stork. So to their little one, they said with a smile that they went to the hospital to pick out "a wonderful baby who looked just like us."

Even small children, however, quickly realize that babies grow inside the tummies of mommies. After a while children wonder how digestion and human development happen in the same stomach, and it works to tell them about a special place inside a mom called the womb. And sooner or later they learn the real story of where babies come from—how they come to be in the womb in the first place.

They have a full explanation of their origins.

If we are going to believe that Jesus came down from heaven, we need a full explanation of His origins. If Jesus had no beginning, then His birth must explain how He could be "born" and yet not have a beginning. The event that students of the Bible call the "virgin birth" of Jesus accomplishes that.

So where did Jesus come from? Let's ask His mother—and several corroborating witnesses. After all, the claim started with Mary's assertion that Jesus wasn't conceived in the usual way: "This is how the birth of Jesus Christ came about: His mother Mary was pledged to be married to Joseph, but before they came together, she was found to be with child through the Holy Spirit" (Matt. 1:18). In other words, Jesus was born to a virgin.

"That's a likely story," cynics say sarcastically. "I have an aunt who swears that's how she got pregnant." Yes, the virgin birth is a startling claim. People have stumbled over this truth for centuries. Yet it's a claim backed by strong evidence.

The best proof for an unusual claim comes from sources that support the claim even against their own best interests. Several sources of evidence had everything to lose by testifying to the truth of the virgin birth:

- *Mary* claimed such an outlandish conception at the risk not only of her own life but of Jesus' life as well. To be pregnant and unmarried exposed her to a "putting away" by Joseph similar to divorce; to be pregnant by a divine miracle exposed her to charges of slandering God. The sentence? Death.

- *Zechariah the priest and his wife, Elizabeth*—the parents of John the Baptizer—celebrated the birth of Jesus as the miraculous birth of the Savior. In a culture that revolved around power and position, it would have been natural for them not to want their son to live in the shadow of Jesus, his younger cousin. They risked shame, social ostracism, and even suicide to stand up for the truth.

- *Jesus' followers and the New Testament authors* risked the rejection of their whole message by claiming a virgin birth, especially since their message had to fulfill perfectly hundreds of prophecies (more on that in a bit). If untrue, the virgin birth was an unnecessary stumbling block. And it would have been easy for Jesus' opponents to discredit the message had the virgin birth not miraculously met the test of the Old Testament.

- Possibly the most astounding endorsement of the virgin birth comes from *Islam,* which for centuries has opposed the Christian gospel. Even the Koran, written six hundred years after Jesus, affirmed His virgin birth (Surah 19:19–21). This would serve Islam no good purpose.

Mary, Joseph, Zechariah, Elizabeth, John, and then the disciples risked everything for what we, too, can accept as truth: Jesus, the man from Nazareth, had His origin in heaven and God Himself as His Father.

For many nonbelievers, the Christian teaching of the virgin birth is so absurd that it unravels everything. If true, however—and I believe the evidence above is powerful—it explains much about Christ. The popular talk-show host Larry King was once asked whom he would interview if he could pick one person

Prophecies Fulfilled by Christ

The virgin birth is all the more amazing because it was predicted hundreds of years in advance by God's Old Testament messengers, the prophets. The Bible foretold with incredible detail facts of the birth, death, and resurrection of Jesus. Here are just a few:

The Bible said the Messiah would:

Prophecy	Predicted	Fulfilled
• be born to the tribe of Judah	Genesis 49:10	Luke 3:33
• be a descendant of David	2 Samuel 7:12ff	Matthew 1:1
• be born to a virgin	Isaiah 7:14	Matthew 1:18ff
• be silent before His accusers	Isaiah 53:7	Matthew 27:12–19
• be pierced in His side	Zechariah 12:10	John 19:34
• rise from the dead	Psalm 16:10	Mark 16:6

Notice a few things: These prophecies were specific. They were fulfilled flawlessly. They were written hundreds of years before Christ. And most were far beyond human ability to control. Of hundreds of biblical prophecies, none is known to be in error. Taken together, they are powerful evidence of the supernatural origin both of Jesus and the Scriptures.

from across history. Mr. King replied that he would like to interview Jesus Christ and that he would ask Him just one question: "Are you indeed virgin born?" "The answer to that question," said Larry King, "would explain history for me."[1]

Prove It to Me, Part 2: The Unblemished Life of Jesus

A second way Jesus proved His roots in heaven—and therefore His absolute and eternal existence—was by displaying purity in a measure only God could possess.

Without a doubt, humanity has regarded the life of Jesus as the purest ever lived. Even at the time of Christ's trial and crucifixion—a circumstance where His enemies should have produced firm proof of His faults—we hear His purity applauded:

- *Pilate*, the Roman ruler who examined Jesus, said to the Jewish priests and an angry crowd, "I have examined him in your presence and have found no basis for your charges against him. Neither has Herod" (Luke 23:14–15).

- *Pilate's wife* sent a message to her husband, "Don't have anything to do with that innocent man" (Matt. 27:19).

- *Judas*, the disciple who betrayed Jesus to the Roman guards, admitted, "I have sinned . . . for I have betrayed innocent blood" (Matt. 27:4). Judas later killed himself out of regret.

- The unnamed *thief* who died on a cross next to Jesus proclaimed, "We are punished justly, for we are getting what our deeds deserve. But this man [Jesus] has done nothing wrong" (Luke 23:41).

Even though the enemies of Jesus tried again and again to bring charges against Him, they were never able to find fault in His pristine life. Jesus reflects the absolute, life-giving purity of God. The Bible puts it this way: "He is the image of the invisible God" (Col. 1:15) and "The Word became flesh and made his dwelling among us. We have seen his glory, the glory of the One and Only, who came from the Father, full of grace and truth" (John 1:14).

No other individual has ever elicited such applause, even from his own followers—including Mohammed (of Islam), Gautama (of Buddhism), and Krishna (of Hinduism). Their lives and their struggles are recorded within their own scriptures. In contrast, in the life of Jesus there was never even a hint that He was ever driven by sinful sensuality or that He needed forgiveness for anything. Jesus alone shines as the spotless One, unblemished by sin.

Jesus wasn't just another good man. Jesus stands heads higher than His religious rivals. He is, in fact, in a class by Himself.

Among Muslims today, the belief is widespread that all of the prophets of Islam were sinless. That purity, however, is hardly the picture presented by Islam's scriptures, the Koran. Nor are the gods of Hinduism or Buddhism without major blemishes:

- The greatest of Islam's prophets, Mohammed, was told to ask for forgiveness for sin (Surahs 47–48), though the word is translated as "faults" rather than "sin." But what is a "fault" that needs forgiving?

- Mohammed's marriages to eleven wives have been a fascinating subject for Muslim teachers to explain. That certainly doesn't prove perfection.

- Muslims also struggle with the embarrassing Koranic description of heaven as "wine and women" (Surah 78:32).

- The shortcomings of Abraham and Moses, two of the most revered prophets in Islam, are plainly stated in the Koran.

Moses asked for forgiveness after slaying the Egyptian (Surah 28,16), and Abraham asked for forgiveness on the Day of Judgment (Surah 26,82).

- Hinduism isn't exempt from scrutiny. The playfulness of Krishna and his exploits with the milkmaids in the Bhagavad-Gita—one of Hinduism's most sacred writings—is frankly an embarrassment to many Hindu teachers.

- The fact that Buddha endured rebirths implies—by every rule of Buddhist belief—a series of imperfect lives. And he left his home in the palace, turning his back on his wife and son, in search of an answer he didn't have. At best, he followed a *path* to purity. He didn't possess purity itself.

The difference between Jesus and Mohammed wasn't just evident in the way they lived but in the way they understood their call. When Mohammed first claimed to have received spiritual revelations, he was confused. He wasn't sure what they meant. It took others to tell him he might be hearing the voice of God. In contrast, Jesus knew exactly who He was and where He came from.

A Globe Full of Gods

Can you see how the claims of Jesus present us with a choice? We can study them, digest them, even debate them before we accept them—or we can fill our cart elsewhere in the supermarket of spiritual truth.

The supermarket presents many options. But that doesn't mean the other options are a better choice.

You might be surprised to learn that Jesus' claim to be God is rare. History doesn't have a long list of people who make sane, serious claims to be God.

Learning About World Religions

You might be confused by the references in *Jesus Among Other Gods* to faiths such as Hinduism, Buddhism, and Islam—but it's crucial to have a fair understanding of other truth claims. Here is a brief overview of these three systems of belief:

Hinduism

Hinduism is a varied system of religion, philosophy, and cultural practices born in India. Hindus share a core belief in reincarnation and a supreme being of many forms and natures.

- Hinduism dates to 1500 B.C. as a system of ritual and multiple gods (polytheism).
- Few practices or beliefs are shared by all Hindus. Shiva, Vishnu, Kali or Ganish are among the most popular deities, but they also worship countless millions of additional minor gods tied to a particular village or family.
- Hinduism is a very complex system where popular practice and philosophical theory do not always meet.
- Hinduism holds that opposing religious theories are aspects of one eternal truth.
- The goal of Hinduism is liberation from ignorance to achieve Moksha Nirvana, a release from rebirths, and a merging with the Oneness of the universe.
- Hinduism holds that human life is a cycle of reincarnation.
- To Hindus, the circumstances of the new birth are determined by the good and evil of past actions.
- Hindus believe the rebirth can be affected by

atonement, rituals, a working out through punishment or reward, and renunciation of worldly desires.

- The self is ultimately divinized in Hinduism.
- The earliest and primary Hindu scriptures are known as the "Vedas."
- The vast majority of the world's three-quarter billion Hindus live in India.

Buddhism

Buddhism is a religion of great variation, yet its central teachings are that suffering is an inherent part of life and that liberation from suffering comes from moral and mental self-purification.

- Buddhism grew out of the teachings of Siddhartha Guatama (563–483 B.C.), who later became known as Buddha, "the enlightened one."
- Buddha is revered not as God but as a spiritual master who points the way to enlightenment.
- At the core of Buddha's teaching are four basic or "noble" truths: (1) life is suffering, (2) the cause of suffering is desire, (3) suffering can be ended by getting rid of desire, and (4) freedom from desire is achieved via an eightfold path of right views, right intention, right speech, right action, right livelihood, right effort, right-mindedness, and right contemplation.
- The goal of Buddhism is to be freed from the cycle of death and rebirth.
- A Buddhist who ceases to desire is "Enlightened" and achieves the state of Nirvana, an abstract nothingness.

- There is no real self in Buddhism.
- Buddhism, strongest in eastern and central Asia, has some three hundred million adherents.
- Buddhism is uncertain about the existence of a personal God.

Islam

Islam teaches that there is one God, Allah. It focuses on submission to God and acceptance of Mohammed as the chief and last prophet of God.

- Islam was founded in Arabia by Mohammed (c. A.D. 570–632). A person who practices Islam is known as a Muslim.
- Islam takes its name from the Arabic word for "devout submission to the will of God."
- Muslims accept their scriptures, the Koran, as the speech of God to Mohammed, and they believe that God Himself is the author.
- Muslims observe the five "pillars" of Islam: (1) the declaration of faith, (2) prayer, (3) fasting, (4) giving alms, and (5) a pilgrimage to Mecca.
- Islam has more than one billion adherents from Africa to the Middle East and parts of Asia and Europe.
- Many predominantly Muslim nations have closed their borders to Christian missionaries or made evangelism illegal.
- Islam sees Jesus as one of the major prophets, but to call Jesus God's Son is blasphemous. It accepts as genuine some of the miracles of Jesus, including the virgin birth and even His power to raise the dead.

What history does provide, however, is a huge assortment of gods manufactured by humans. That list is endless. In one sense, in fact, "God" is whatever person or entity you credit with being the ultimate power in this universe—the One through whom the universe came to be, and the One to whom the universe answers. You can spot whether something is your "god" by the way you live and by the values you hold even if you don't live by them. Your "god" is whatever you treat as ultimately good and ultimately powerful. It could be a way of living, a practice, a ritual, an idea, a purported spiritual entity, or even yourself.

Here's the problem: You can choose an alleged god but miss the genuine God.

Getting the Real Thing

I want us to connect with the God who is real—the God who has revealed Himself in Jesus Christ.

I once stood at the side of a road, watching the golden statue of a "god" being transported from one temple to another. Thousands clamored to give an offering and to receive a blessing. The priests accompanying the god had incense and ash in their hands and generously distributed the deity's goodwill on any fruit or piece of clothing placed before them. The sight was extraordinary. Rich, poor, young, and old stretched up their hands as this chariot crawled by. I asked a woman who had just received her "blessing" if this god actually existed—or if he were just an expression of some inner hunger. She hesitated and then said, "If you think in your heart that he exists, then he does."

"What if you do not believe he exists?" I asked.

"Then he doesn't exist," she softly said.

God isn't merely whatever we hope "he" or "she" or "it" is. I think each of us wants to build life on more than a wish. We can't depend on a figment of our imagination. We can't find friendship with God if the "god" we believe in doesn't actually exist.

We are only at the beginning of examining the reality of Christ and the absolute truth of His claims. Let's search out some more—to see not only that Jesus is indeed God but that He is the kind of God to whom we want to give our lives.

THREE

HOW DO WE KNOW THE CLAIMS OF JESUS ARE TRUE?

Some years ago, I was staying at a small hotel in the Philippines. The woman who managed the place had a graduate degree in philosophy, and we launched into a long conversation on whether it made sense to believe in God. She asked if I had met a family at the hotel who had come from Australia to have their son cured of cancer by a faith healer.

One evening I was invited to this couple's room. Their ten- or twelve-year-old son lay in his narrow bed, wasted with illness. He was motionless. Pitiful. His gray face was drawn with the look of death. On a table near his side was a jar with some murky liquid and a frightful-looking, purple, fleshly mass that sprouted hairy roots.

His parents and I talked in whispers. The boy's mother pointed to the jar and said to me, "Do you see what is in that jar?"

I nodded.

"That's the cancer the faith healer removed without surgery. It's like magic! We're sure our son is healed."

The family was in terrible pain. Yet it was extremely difficult to look into the eyes of parents who were willing to trust their child's life to such a "healer." Despite clear evidence that their son was dying, these two educated and well-to-do people raved about his cure—a cure brought about by a man who muttered a prayer, made no incision, and yet, they said, pulled this fist-sized thing that was "the cancer" from their son.

How can you explain this ability to believe the bizarre?

Is Your Faith Blind?

The gentle question I put to those parents was this: "Would you write me within a month or two," I asked, "and tell me if your son has been truly healed? My work takes me all over the world, and it would really help me to know if the power of that healer is real." They took my address and eagerly promised to write. That was more than a decade ago. I have never heard from them.

> To commit your life, habits, thoughts, goals, and priorities—*everything*—to a certain set of beliefs without asking and answering questions is to build your life on a flimsy foundation.

Given less fragile circumstances, most of us would have tough questions for those parents—and for the alleged healer. We would jump at the chance to test the reality of that healer's power. But think about this: How do you feel when someone turns the tables on you and questions the reality of Jesus' claims? Nervous? Confident? Annoyed? However you feel, you can't dodge that challenge, because to many non-Christians, faith in a Jesus who performed miracles and rose from the dead is just as bizarre as trust in a man who claims to extract tumors barehanded.

We live in a world overflowing with contradicting ways of defining "ultimate reality"—the facts of the nature of the universe, whether God exists, and so on. We live in a sometimes-hostile society where antagonists will topple our beliefs if they aren't rock solid.

Moreover, we each have questions to settle for ourselves. You might not have the struggles I shared in the first chapter. You could have an entirely different set of questions you would like to ask God face to face. But to commit your life, habits, thoughts, goals, and priorities—*everything*—to a certain set of beliefs without asking and answering questions is to build your life on a flimsy foundation. Think about it: The risk you take on God is even larger than trusting your physical life to a fake healer. After all, Jesus insists that He is the only true answer to your life's whole purpose and eternal destiny.

Some believers think non-Christians who question Jesus are evil—and that Christians who ask for explanations are unspiritual. I think, though, that we are foolish to trust God unless we can thoroughly test and verify His claims.

Thinking Hard About What You Believe

Sooner or later in school, you will run into the writings of Bertrand Russell (1872–1970), a British philosopher and mathematician famous for his biting comments on religion. Someone once asked the well-known atheist, "If you meet God after you die, what will you say to Him to justify your unbelief?"

"I will tell Him that He did not give me enough evidence," Russell snapped.

Bertrand Russell might have been an unusually loud and hostile critic of religious belief—and Christianity in particular—but his thirst for proof isn't unique. You wouldn't have to look far to find each of these skeptics in your life:

- a science buff who says the facts of evolution disprove the Bible,

- a friend's mom who rejects God because her father abused her,

- a family member who can't believe in God because He "didn't answer my prayers,"

- a peer who says nothing exists beyond what we can taste, smell, hear, touch, or see, or

- a teacher who deliberately builds a system of right and wrong apart from the teachings of Scripture.

Loudly or quietly, these critics express their doubts. You might or might not be able to help them past their misgivings about the Christian message. But unbelief is contagious; it's easy to catch if you don't think hard about what you believe—and why.

Why Christians Run from Thinking Hard

To be honest, I wonder more about people who *don't* want reasons for what they believe than about those who *do*. I have met thousands of people who have made wholehearted commitments to ghastly "gods" and "goddesses." I'm shocked that they never question their beliefs. But I find that Christians run away from debate for many reasons:

- *Finding hard-nosed reasons for belief can be hard work.* Did I admit that? The search for truth can be intense but rewarding. There is an old adage that says, "It is better to debate a question before settling it than to settle a question before debating it."

- *Exploring questions can be hazardous to your spiritual health.* That's only half-true. Entertaining struggles with

Who Are These Wise Guys?

It might be tempting to paint Christianity's critics as "idiots" or "infidels." In the short run, those *ad hominem* ("against the man") attacks might sound smart, but they don't prove or disprove anything. And in the long run, they destroy your own credibility.

Christianity's opponents say genuinely wise and witty things. Ponder these thoughts from Bertrand Russell:

- *On the importance of scientific observation:* "Aristotle could have avoided the mistake of thinking that women have fewer teeth than men, by the simple device of asking Mrs. Aristotle to keep her mouth open while he counted."
- *On why people cling to crazy beliefs:* "Man is a credulous [gullible] animal, and must believe *something*; in the absence of good grounds for belief, he will be satisfied with bad ones."

In the voices of skeptics you can also hear pain— pain that can be a starting point to talk about the message of God's love. One more from Russell:

- *On the agonies of life:* "The life of man is a long march through the night, surrounded by invisible foes, tortured by weariness and pain, towards a goal that few can hope to reach, and where none may tarry long."[1]

faith has caused many to struggle more. But countless Christians have found that the only path to spiritual maturity is to push through their questions to find God's answers. My own intellectual battles were unavoidable in a land filled with as many gods as people.

- *Maybe we won't find answers.* I beg to differ. People hostile to belief in God often label faith as a mindless trap, a lure for the emotions. They don't believe that faith can sustain the weight not only of our emotions but of our minds. I promise you this: You will never hear a challenging question so radically new that it hasn't already been asked and adequately answered.

- *The digital culture that surrounds us doesn't encourage reasoning.* I think it's more accurate to say that new technologies emphasize different types of learning. In Asia, I recently saw a video game that required players to dance on the floor to move the controls. Phenomenal! It's just another sign that your generation will learn much more visually and numerically. But you still need to learn to work with words and ideas and to evaluate arguments and logic.

- *We aren't smart enough.* That's absolutely false. I realize we are all built with different abilities. But don't be afraid of material that seems over your head. You *do* have the ability to grapple with it! Don't say, "This is too hard for me."

When you were younger, standing on your tiptoes to reach a cookie jar didn't make you any taller. Dealing with ideas is amazingly different. Stretching your understanding makes you that much taller—that much smarter—for your next intellectual reach.

Aren't We Just Supposed to Believe?

Some Christians distrust thinking. They don't like to entertain questions of faith. And they might distance themselves from schools that don't teach precisely what they want taught. It can all add up to a belief that brainwork is bad.

We do have to keep watch over our minds. The Bible does say this:

> For the message of the cross is foolishness to those who are perishing, but to us who are being saved it is the power of God. For it is written: "I will destroy the wisdom of the wise; the intelligence of the intelligent I will frustrate." Where is the wise man? Where is the scholar? Where is the philosopher of this age? Has not God made foolish the wisdom of the world? (1 Cor. 1:18–20)

We need to check the context of those verses and others like them. This particular one is about "perishing" people—people who don't believe the message of the cross. The point of the passage? For those who deny Christ, intellectual ability can actually hinder the search for spiritual truth. It doesn't rule out those who believe in Christ using their intelligence to serve the God who is ultimate truth and ultimate wisdom.

There is a better way to think about our minds: The Bible calls us to renew our minds to think like He thinks, not to surgically remove them (Rom. 12:1–2).

Be encouraged that the Bible is full of people who thought hard. Some even debated with God, yet they weren't struck by lightning or otherwise divinely punished:

- Moses questioned whether God had made the right choice in appointing him to free the Israelite slaves in Egypt (Exod. 3:11).
- Habakkuk looked at rampant evil and suffering in the world and yelled at God, "How long?" (Hab. 1:2ff).
- Nathanael freely expressed his jaded opinion about Jesus' roots (John 1:46).
- Thomas was permitted to see and touch Christ's wounds in order to believe Christ had risen from the dead (John 20:24–29).
- The Bereans took time to test even the apostle Paul's teaching against Scripture (Acts 17:11).

The Prime of Your Life

You don't get a driver's license until you are sixteen. You likely won't graduate from high school until you are eighteen. You can't be a fighter pilot until you are in your twenties or a full-fledged doctor until you are pushing thirty. But right now you are at the prime of your life to seek answers to spiritual questions. It's how God designed you.

You see, childhood starts with faith. A child's mind has only a tiny capacity to grasp the *reason* for its trust. But when she nestles on her mother's shoulder or leaps into her father's arms, she does so because of a *trust* that those shoulders will bear her and that those arms will catch her.

But over time, that child's faith is tested. The character of her parent will either prove her trust to be wise or foolish. Trust is sustained by thinking through that trust. In the same way, mature spiritual faith isn't empty of *reasons* for faith.

Burying the Evidence

People like Bertrand Russell contend that there are no solid reasons for belief in the absolute truth of Jesus' claims. Interestingly enough, the Bible has a staggering response. The Scriptures say that it isn't the *absence* of evidence that baffles some doubters; it is, rather, their *suppression* of the evidence.

You might have a relative who has visited the doctor and been told, "I have bad news: Your cholesterol is through the roof, and you are at grave risk of a heart attack. But I have good news: If you follow my instructions, we can take care of the problem."

> Trust is sustained by thinking through that trust. Mature spiritual faith isn't empty of *reasons* for faith.

Some people swallow hard and make the changes necessary to live. Yet others plug their ears to that news. They don't want to exercise. They don't want to eat right. They deny all the evidence that supports what the doctor says because they don't want to follow the doctor's orders.

Some people refuse to believe in God because admitting He exists means having to answer to their Creator. The same people reject Jesus because receiving the good news of Christ means accepting a set of instructions to agree with God about sin and to allow Christ to be Master of their lives.

The Bible diagnoses the disease of unbelief like this:

- "For since the creation of the world God's invisible qualities—his eternal power and divine nature—have been clearly seen, being understood from what has been made, so that men are without excuse" (Rom. 1:20).

- "This is the verdict: Light has come into the world, but men loved darkness instead of light because their deeds were evil. Everyone who does evil hates the light, and will not come into the light for fear that his deeds will be exposed. But whoever lives by the truth comes into the light" (John 3:19–21).

The truth of God calls people to account, and some people find all sorts of ways to suppress the evidence for truth rather than to live with its implications.

"I Don't Want There to Be a God"

There are honest doubters. And then there are doubters who *won't* believe. After years of wrestling with these issues, I have seen this proven time and again. Read carefully these words of Thomas Nagel, professor of philosophy at New York University. This is how he explains his deep-seated dislike of religion:

> In speaking of the fear of religion, I don't mean to refer to the entirely reasonable hostility toward certain established religions . . . in virtue of their objectionable moral doctrines, social policies, and political influence. Nor am I referring to the association of many religious beliefs with superstition and the acceptance of evident empirical falsehoods. I am talking about something much deeper—namely the fear of religion itself. . . . I want atheism to be true and am made uneasy by the fact that some of the most intelligent and well informed people I know are religious believers. *It isn't just that I don't believe in God and*

naturally, hope there is no God! I don't want there to be a God;
I don't want the universe to be like that.[2] (emphasis added)

Nagel can find all kinds of reasons to reject religion. I would agree that Christianity has all sorts of noxious, unbiblical attachments that have nothing to do with Jesus. But, Nagel admits, his biggest roadblock to faith is that he doesn't *want* there to be a God.

That is blatant, committed unbelief: "I don't want there to be a God." While Bertrand Russell's skepticism may be understood as the honest search of reason, we had better be sure that his is not actually the deliberate unbelief of Thomas Nagel lurking beneath an intellectual quest. In reality, that kind of skepticism is a warping of reason, hiding a bad case of close-mindedness. The bottom line is this: *To that frame of mind, nothing would serve as sufficient evidence.* That's a problem. It is, in fact, the problem Jesus addressed in our next encounter.

Jesus Didn't Run from Questions

In our next encounter, the most religious people of Jesus' day demanded evidence for who He claimed to be. But like modern skeptics such as Russell or Nagel, they didn't actually want the answer He gave them.

In John 2:12–25, we see Jesus like we have never seen Him. His actions and His words shocked onlookers. He denounced the powerbrokers of religion. He referred to the temple as His Father's house. And He made a claim unmatched in the history of religion.

It happened like this:

When it was almost time for the Jewish Passover, Jesus went up to Jerusalem. In the temple courts he found men selling cattle, sheep and doves, and others sitting at tables exchanging money. So he made a whip out of cords, and drove all from the temple area, both sheep and cattle; he scattered the coins of the money changers and overturned their tables. To those who sold doves he said, "Get these out of here! How dare you turn my Father's house into a market!" His disciples remembered that it is written: "Zeal for your house will consume me." (John 2:13–17)

The disciples remembered the Old Testament prophecy that concern for the purity of God's house, the temple, would drive the Messiah (Ps. 69:9). Still, the boldness of Jesus must have made them nervous.

And certainly the boldness of Jesus made the religious leaders furious. His antagonists couldn't contain their rage. They demanded Jesus give them a sign to justify His daring action: "What miraculous sign can you show us to prove your authority to do all this?" (John 2:18). What they wanted to know, in other words, was "How are You going to prove Yourself to us? How do we know You are who You claim to be?"

Jesus knew that their question was anything but a quest for truth. But He offered proof that no other person claiming Messianic or divine office has ever fulfilled. To so great a challenge, Jesus offered an unparalleled demonstration of power: "Destroy this temple, and I will raise it again in three days" (v. 19).

"What?" they countered. They assumed He referred to the magnificent building in which they stood. "It has taken forty-six years to build this temple, and you are going to raise it in three days?" His claim sounded absurd to them. Jesus might as well have said, "I am an alien, and I am going to fly my spaceship from earth to another galaxy and back in a record-breaking three-day time."

But Jesus wasn't talking about a *building*. He spoke of His *body*. For all to hear, He had predicted that He would die and

What's So Bad About Belief?

Thomas Nagel neatly summarized reasons people object to Christianity and other religions, and in conversations with your non-Christian friends you are likely to hear more or less the same list. Sometimes what critics assume is genuine Christianity is really excess or even blatant sin. At other times they dislike something that is essential to our faith. But here are the problems they see:

- "Moral doctrines"—the fact that Christians claim the Bible's commands are intended for everyone
- "Social policies"—the way Christians press their beliefs in public on issues such as abortion
- "Political influence"—the clout Christians wield in the political process, particularly the church's abuse of power in the Middle Ages, the legalism of the Puritan era, and the heightened involvement in politics by Christians in the past twenty years
- "Superstition"—belief in Satan, demons, angels, and God Himself
- "Empirical falsehoods"—acceptance of supposedly anything outside the reach of the scientific method, anything believed to be supernatural or miraculous

rise again after three days. John adds, "The temple he had spoken of was his body. After he was raised from the dead, his disciples recalled what he had said. Then they believed the Scripture and the words that Jesus had spoken" (vv. 21–22).

What About All the Hypocrites at Church?

The quest of the religious leaders who challenged Jesus was not for truth. They maintained a colossal system of religion, but they didn't recognize it when God Himself stood among them.

This is hypocrisy—pretending to have a purity or a passion for God you don't actually possess. The presence of hypocrites in any church gives opponents ample opportunity to challenge our faith. It's an enormous stumbling block even to people who would like to believe in Jesus. And it might be a huge challenge to your own faith.

Here are some answers to people who ask, "But what about all the hypocrites in church?"

- *Hypocrisy isn't unique to Christianity.* Sadly, it is easy to find hypocrites in any religion or even the antireligion of atheism. One illustration: Right outside the hotel in a place I visit often is a little shrine. I have watched in the morning as thousands walked by. Most would pause, bow, fold their hands, or make some kind of a reverential sign to honor the deity and then move on. But many of those who ceremoniously carried out that ritual would then walk a few paces and wait to see which tourist they could trick that morning. From unfurling nude pictures or offering the services of a prostitute, to selling fake Rolex watches for twenty dollars, their day was spent in the immoral and the illegal. I have decided that *hypocrite* is a very innocent word to describe these lives. Their activities, both religious and immoral, weren't hidden— they were all done in the open.

- *The Bible's condemnation of the sin of hypocrisy is clear.* By overturning the tables in the temple, Jesus visibly demonstrated His rage against fake spirituality (John 2:12–25). The Bible also clearly pledges that God will judge hypocrites (Matt. 24:51).

- *The Bible teaches that judgment of hypocrites will not be immediate.* Jesus said that "weeds" and "wheat," hypocrites and true believers, would exist side by side until Judgment Day—and He pointed out that uprooting the weeds now often destroys the wheat (Matt. 13:24–30).

- *While we might not like the fact that God is slow to judge, we should all be grateful for His mercy.* Peter writes, "The Lord is not slow in keeping his promise [to return in judgment], as some understand slowness. He is patient with you, not wanting anyone to perish, but everyone to come to repentance" (2 Pet. 3:9).

As a holy God who highly desires a pure people (Titus 2:11–14), God is more angered by hypocrisy than we can ever be.

The Greatest Proof of All

What greater proof could Jesus offer than to rise from the dead? Jesus' fulfillment of His promise to rise from the dead is unique. No other major world religion boasts the resurrection of its leader. Nor do the obscure religions that claim what students of religion call a "resurrection myth" root their stories in historical fact.

Atheism, however, rails against this central claim of our faith: "Christ couldn't have risen from the dead!" What we see, however, is that atheists seldom interact with the evidence Christians offer as proof of the resurrection. The argument of the atheist is that God or the resurrection is totally outside the realm of the *believable* because, after all, nothing exists outside the realm of the *quantifiable*—in other words, apart from the natural world we can study with science and math.

Their arguments spring up like dandelions year after year, looking just the same. A recent article by Matthew Parris in the *Times* of London called "The Rage of Reason" is typical of a thinker who claims that he loves reason—and that Christians love irrationality. After pleading for atheists of the past like Bertrand Russell to return and save us from "religious non-sense," Parris offers this test of truth from David Hume, another famous thinker you will run into in philosophy class:

> If we take in our hand any volume: of divinity or school of meta-physics, for instance; let us ask, *Does it contain any abstract reasoning concerning quantity or number?* No. *Does it contain any experimental reasoning concerning matter of fact and existence?* No. Commit it then to the flames; For it can contain nothing but sophistry and illusion.[3]

Parris thinks that Hume has delivered a devastating, knock-out punch to religion, so that it now lies unconscious on the floor before the stupendous stature of science. If you can't hold God in your hand, Hume is saying, then you have no facts to hang on to. If a statement doesn't fit mathematics ("quantity or number") or science ("fact and existence"), then it must be tossed "into the flames."

The only problem with this test of truth is that *Hume's test itself doesn't pass the test*. David Hume's grand declaration isn't scientific, and it isn't mathematical. If a statement must be either produced by math or verified by science to be true, then David

How Scientific Is Science?

I was having dinner with a few scholars, most of whom were scientists, when our discussion veered into the conflict between science's starting point—nature alone—and supernaturalism's starting point, God as the only sufficient explanation for our origin.

I asked them a question that might be useful to you in science class. "If the big bang were indeed where it all began—which one can fairly well grant, at least to this point in science's thinking—may I ask what preceded the big bang?" Their answer, which I had anticipated, was that the universe was shrunk down to a singularity.

I pursued, "But isn't it correct that a singularity as defined by science is a point at which all the laws of physics break down?"

"That is correct," was the answer.

"Then, technically, your starting point is not scientific either."

There was silence. Their expressions showed their minds were scurrying for an escape hatch.

They didn't find one.

Hume's statement itself must be false.

It's like that story you might have read as a child: The emperor has no clothes, while boasting the finest threads.

Personalizing the Proof

We can't run away from the question of opponents or doubts of our own. Truth seekers are justified in wanting to know what distinguishes faith from foolishness or irrationality, especially when it seems no coherent logic is ever offered for "faith."

But was Jesus implying that belief is nothing more than blind commitment? Something you force from your brain by an act of the will? I think not. He did say, in effect, that if you test His claims by the same measure that you verify other facts, you will find Him and His teaching thoroughly trustworthy. There is ample evidence for Christ's claims, so the denial of Christ has little to do with facts and much to do with the bent of a person who has already decided to resist truth.

> Jesus said, in effect, that if you test His claims by the same measure that you verify other facts, you will find Him and His teaching thoroughly trustworthy.

Each individual who comes into this kind of faith in the one true God does so through a different struggle. On one hand, Moses was the classic Old Testament example of how faith was built into someone who found trusting God difficult. God pursued Moses long and hard until he understood that the God he served expected his trust and that He would prove Himself. Abraham, on the other hand, so hungered after God that he was willing with minimal outward proof to leave home to follow God.

What both brands of faith have in common, though, is both *trust* and *substance*. Jesus claimed to be God in human flesh. The true believer *trusts* Him to be speaking the truth. But everything He said and did offers *substance*. It explains and supports that claim. And nothing Jesus said or did undermines trust. It's been said that human nature abhors a vacuum, and that must be true of our faith too. None of us lives comfortably with a vacuous faith, what we might call an "airhead" approach to spiritual things.

So what substance does our faith have? If the resurrection is the greatest proof of Christ's claims, how do we prove the resurrection?

Putting Christ's Claim to the Test

Christians have real reasons to regard the resurrection as a real event in history. Jesus gave us an ultimate test of His claim: "Destroy this temple, and I will raise it again in three days."

Could He really have done what He promised? Look at the facts:

- Jesus would have been foolish to make a claim so far beyond any natural happening and, if false, so easy to disprove. Predicting a spiritual resurrection would have been an easy way out, because even a corpse can be supposedly "spiritually resurrected." Jesus predicted a *physical,* verifiable rising from the dead.

- Jesus gave enormous proof of His authority by accurately predicting His death and the time of His bodily resurrection. The fulfillment of that prediction reveals the uniqueness of Jesus above all contenders.

- After Jesus was laid in the tomb, the temple leaders needed only to produce His body to disprove His claim that He would rise again on the third day. But they could not. The absence of Jesus' body proved precisely that He did what He said He would.

- Christ's body was sealed in the tomb by a huge stone and guarded by soldiers of the greatest power on earth at the time—the Roman Empire. For the disciples to have stolen the body so they could claim Jesus had risen is like claiming you and your friends could penetrate the Pentagon.

- Hundreds of eyewitnesses saw Jesus after the resurrection (1 Cor. 15:6), enough credible testimony to overwhelm any court of law.

- Opponents of the resurrection must explain what other event could have caused such a radical spiritual and psychological change in the followers of Jesus. Having seen the risen Christ, once-frightened disciples began a worldwide movement. An encounter with the resurrected Jesus turned a murderer named Saul of Tarsus into the apostle Paul.

- Jesus' followers were immediately subject to persecution and death for their belief. It is hard to believe that Jesus' inner circle of eyewitnesses—who would have known had the story been concocted—would die for a lie.

- And an argument often ignored, one that takes into account the culture of the Middle East: If the resurrection were not true, the disciples *themselves* would have concocted the idea of a spiritual resurrection. This approach would have spared their lives. It would have spared them from shame—"saved face." And had the authorities produced Christ's body, it still would have spared their message from disproof.

Millions upon millions of reasonable, intelligent people have found the physical resurrection of Jesus the most plausible explanation of the facts, finding not just an explanation of the past but a hope for the present and future. Jesus demonstrated that death has been conquered. Paul himself said that if Christ was not raised from the dead, our hope in Him is pointless and "we are to be pitied more than all men" (1 Cor. 15:19).

What More Proof Do We Want?

The fact that we have a reasonable mind to ask and answer these questions is a miracle in and of itself. Isn't that another proof of God's reality? The fact that God allows us to pursue our questions is one of His greatest gifts to us. Isn't that another proof of God's reliability?

The faith that the Bible teaches isn't opposed to reason. It isn't ignorant belief in something that has been proven false. It isn't an attempt to force-fit every piece of information into the mold of our wishes. Biblical faith is based on the knowledge that the One in whom we place our faith has proven He is worthy of that trust. At its core, faith is a confidence in the person of Jesus Christ and in His power, so that even when His power doesn't serve my goals or my whims, I am still confident in Him be-cause of who He is.

> The Christian's faith isn't a leap into the dark. It is a well-placed trust in the Light of the world, Jesus.

If we believe Christ is who He says He is, we trust. Out of love, we commit both our minds and hearts to Him. Based on all that Christ has demonstrated Himself to be, that is not a crazy response.

Faith in Jesus Christ is a thoughtful, passionate, and moral commitment to a truth that stands up under the scrutiny of the mind, the heart, and the conscience. Christians aren't bumping around in the darkness of unreason; those who see the facts and steel themselves not to believe are. The prophecies, person, and work of Christ; His resurrection from the dead; and many other pieces of evidence can be confirmed in history. The skeptic doesn't deal with these.

This is why Jesus challenged the idea that more evidence would have generated more faith. The Christian writer George MacDonald said long ago that to give truth to a person who does not love the truth is to only give more reasons for misinterpretation.

The Christian's faith isn't a leap into the dark. It is a well-placed trust in the Light of the world, Jesus.

FOUR

WON'T JESUS MAKE LIFE WONDERFUL?

When Megan was four, her parents were killed in a plane crash. With no relatives willing to take her in, Megan was placed in a shelter along with a dozen other girls waiting for adoption. Megan had a meager life—her clothes were threadbare, her food was skimpy and tasteless, and adult attention almost always harsh.

Several years went by. One day, Megan was whisked away to a better place. A childless couple who had made billions on software welcomed her into their home, where they and their dozens of staff tended her every need. Megan had more than she could ever imagine—fresh clothes, abundant toys, a gourmet children's menu at every meal, splashy parties at her own indoor water park, and access to her loving parents at any moment.

Megan is imaginary, but you could probably fill out the facts and feelings of her story. She is a modern "little orphan Annie," as in the musical that has been remade and restaged again and again. You probably know that in that classic, Annie, after her adoption by Daddy Warbucks, lacks nothing. But unlike the evil adults in the story who plot to swindle money from Warbucks, Annie is pure. She wants nothing but a relationship with her new father.

Will the Sun Come Out Tomorrow?

How would we react if we were suddenly thrust from poverty to plenty? We might be tempted to live by the pool, sampling hors d'oeuvres, rather than getting to know our new family. We might focus on the parties and miss the fact that we finally have parents. We might take advantage of the situation and *demand* that the sun come out today, tomorrow, and every day—to stretch a line from Annie.

Our situation when we encounter Jesus is much the same:

We are poor.

He is rich.

There is a genuine possibility that we might focus on the gifts rather than the Giver.

Our human tendency to pursue the good things God can give us instead of pursuing God Himself is at the heart of the next question people put to Jesus.

Jesus the Wonder Worker

John 6 tells us that one day when Jesus saw a throng of people approaching, He asked His disciple Philip where they should buy bread for everyone to eat. The disciples turned the pockets of their tunics inside out and said, "Lunch for five thousand? We don't have that kind of money! Eight months' salary would barely give each one a bite!"

But Jesus already had a plan.

You have to wonder why Simon Peter shuffled toward Jesus with a boy holding five small loaves of bread and two small fish, but he did. Here's what happened:

> Jesus said, "Have the people sit down." There was plenty of grass in that place, and the men sat down, about five thousand of

them. Jesus then took the loaves, gave thanks, and distributed to those who were seated as much as they wanted. He did the same with the fish.

When they had all had enough to eat, he said to his disciples, "Gather the pieces that are left over. Let nothing be wasted." So they gathered them and filled twelve baskets with the pieces of the five barley loaves left over by those who had eaten. (John 6:10–13)

The miracle Jesus performed was so astounding that the people wanted to crown Him king. He pulled away from the crowds, but they soon chased Him down. Jesus had quick insight into their motives, which He spoke out loud: "You're looking for Me because you want more bread!" He told the people to set their sights on more important things. They would be better off focusing less on their stomachs and more on spiritual things—like obeying God by believing in Him: "Do not work for food that spoils," He said, "but for food that endures to eternal life, which the Son of Man will give you" (v. 27).

> If God is real, isn't He supposed to make our lives wonderful?

But they countered Jesus with an objection: "Our forefathers ate the manna in the desert. . . . What will you do?" (vv. 31, 30)

You might remember how the Israelites had escaped slavery in Egypt and then wandered in the desert. God had rained down food for their ancestors to eat for *forty years*. It was monotonous but nevertheless miraculous. And it was easier than hunting or gathering or farming. Morning by morning the Israelites gathered a snowy white morsel they simply called "manna," a Hebrew word that literally means, "What is it?" (Exod. 16:31).

What Do You Say to People Who Don't Believe the Bible?

To some people, the miracle accounts in the Bible are fairy tales, stories the disciples of Jesus wrote down to make their dead leader look good. It doesn't help much to argue about the believability of an individual miracle. It's more beneficial to talk about the larger issue of the Bible's reliability.

Christians believe that God revealed Himself not merely in a book but through Christ, who is God "incarnate" or "in human flesh" (John 1:14). We believe the Bible is an accurate record of that supreme revelation of God for a number of reasons. When you meet someone who struggles with the Bible in any area, you can respectfully share these points:

- The Bible was written by forty different authors over a period of more than fifteen hundred years. It contains discussions of hundreds of subjects and is written in a dozen literary styles. Yet its contents show amazing unity—a unity that would not be seen, for example, if we compiled a book on medicine by forty different authors spanning fifteen hundred years.

- The Bible is "God-breathed" (2 Tim. 3:16). That's different from saying it was dictated by God, the claim made by Islam about the Koran. "God-breathed" means that, by the Holy Spirit, God directed what was to be written (2 Pet. 1:21). The authors of Scripture claimed to speak God's words. "God-breathed" means God worked through human authors in a way that allowed for their personal styles and vocabularies, a characteristic obvious in Scripture.

- In its hundreds of detailed, accurate prophecies, the Bible displays a completely unique knowledge of the future impossible to explain apart from God.

- Christians believe the Bible is error-free, perfect truth. That isn't the same as perfect in literary beauty. Mohammed claimed the Koran was a beautifully written book, flawless in its beauty.

- The events of the Bible are rooted in the real world— and the accuracy of the geography and history of the Bible has been extensively confirmed.

- The Bible has been accurately transmitted since its writing. The degree of accuracy in the copies we have of the New Testament exceeds 99 percent, which is greater than that of any other ancient book. The reason? We have far more manuscripts from the Bible than for other ancient books, and those manuscripts were copied much closer in time to the originals than manuscripts we possess for other books.

- The Bible was written by people who were willing to die for its truth. Norman Geisler writes, "People sometimes die for what they believe to be true and isn't. But few are willing to die for what they know to be false."[1] The early disciples clearly were in a position to know whether their message was true or false.

Once we are convinced that the Bible is an accurate book, then we can address the plausibility of the miraculous as well as the message taught by individual miracles.

> It's also fair to invite the Bible's challengers to explore the Bible's life-changing message for themselves. Many who belittle the Bible have never read it.

What Jesus' hearers said was both a challenge and a plea: *If You are really God, aren't You supposed to drop food from the sky for us? Aren't You supposed to make our lives wonderful?*

The Jesus-Chasing Crowd

We need to notice something. The crowd didn't chase down Jesus without reason. They had figured out that bread wasn't the only thing Jesus could provide. Jesus had proven His power to work a variety of miracles:

- He had changed water into wine at a wedding feast. Jesus revealed His *power over the elements* (John 2:1–11).

- He had healed a paralytic by the Bethesda pool and the dying son of a royal official. Jesus showed His *power over sickness* (John 4:43–5:14).

- He had multiplied that young lad's lunch to feed thousands. Jesus displayed His *power over all provision* (John 6:1–15).

- He had walked on water and met up with His disciples in the middle of the Sea of Galilee. Jesus exerted His *power over natural law* (John 6:16–24).

Can you see what they saw? Jesus had power over every facet of life. If we slip on the sandals of these Bible folk and ponder what they had witnessed, we can dream up all kinds of things God could provide. We could enlist Jesus to rearrange our world and to fix all sorts of situations, both major and minor. We could ask Him for:

- healing for the brain tumor growing in the head of a fourth-grade neighbor,

- a new sports car,

- lots of friends,

- a job for an unemployed parent,

- a fresh start for parents headed for divorce,

- free tickets to the movies this Friday night, or

- a complete wardrobe overhaul.

God is glad to meet our needs, but the crowd around Jesus had a serious problem.

It's not too hard to discern that some in the crowd were beginning to eye Jesus as if He were a candy or soda machine that delivered free goods, no coins required: Push a button, and out pops a treat! The crowd had seen a boy's lunch feed several thousand people—with baskets full of scraps left over. They had seen a paralytic of nearly four decades suddenly walk again—all because Jesus said, "Pick up your mat and walk." They wanted to know: Is this power transferable? Can it be bought? Having seen the miracles, the crowds wanted to make the most of the situation. They sought the power they assumed would make life more tasty—a miracle-working ability that would ensure, among other things, full stomachs and a limitless supply of bread.

Who could blame them? Who wouldn't want Jesus to be that kind of God? I recently heard a comment from a man who had won an enormous amount of money in a lottery. "What is the biggest difference in your life?" asked an interviewer. "I eat out more often," came the matter-of-fact answer.

Meeting up with God is like being invited into the home of a generous family able to act on their generosity. But the concrete things God provides can distract us from what we really need: spiritual nourishment in the form of a relationship with God.

The Miracles You Never Notice

Skeptics who challenge the truth of miracle stories don't realize miracles exist all around them. Take, for example, those who smirk at His walking on water (John 6:16–24). They forget that what they swallow in a glass of water is a miracle in and of itself!

Think of this for a moment. In eighteen milliliters of water (about two swallows), there are 6×10^{23} molecules of H_2O. How much is 6×10^{23}? A good computer can carry out 10 million counts per second. It would take that computer two billion years to count to 6×10^{23}.

Look at it another way. A stack of five hundred sheets of paper is two to three inches high. How high would the stack be if it had 6×10^{23} sheets? That stack would reach from earth to the sun, not once, but more than one million times. Yet in about two gulps of water, God has packed that many molecules.

I would say that the miracle of walking on water is small for the God who created water in the first place. C. S. Lewis once commented that a slow miracle is no easier to perform than an instant one. What I find truly unbelievable are the explanations skeptics offer for these "slow miracles" of life. I find it infinitely harder to believe that matter appeared out of nothing than that God created the world.

Searching for Sense—and Real Satisfaction

In his book *Into Thin Air,* Jon Krakauer describes the dangers that overcame climbers in an expedition to Mount Everest during the spring of 1996. Their attempt to reach the summit resulted in numerous deaths. Some circumstances were beyond the control of the climbers, but basic mistakes cost them dearly.

One climber who died was Andy Harris. One of the expedition leaders, Harris had stayed at the peak past the deadline the leaders had set. On his trek down, he desperately needed oxygen. Harris radioed his predicament to the base camp, telling them his need and explaining that he had come upon a stack of oxygen canisters left by other climbers—all empty. Climbers who had passed the canisters on their own return from the summit knew that the canisters were full. Even as his friends at the base camp pleaded with him on the radio to use the canisters, Harris continued to argue that the canisters were empty.[2]

Harris was starved for oxygen. The lack of what he needed so disoriented his mind that he didn't realize he was surrounded by fresh supplies. What he held in his hand was absent in his brain. His lack of oxygen destroyed his ability to recognize that his rescue was right in his hand.

What You Get Is Jesus Himself

What oxygen is to the brain, Jesus is to our hearts. He satisfies our deepest longings unlike anything else. And He causes us to think straight.

If we were to list all of our hungers, we might be surprised at how many legitimate hungers we have. We hunger for truth, love, knowledge, belonging, self-expression, justice, imagination, learning, and significance—to name a few. If we browse any library or bookstore, we will soon realize that vast psychological theories have emerged to describe each one of these hungers or needs.

As important and right as those needs are, our need for Jesus is infinitely greater. A few verses after the passage you read above, Jesus put an exclamation point on His supreme place in our lives and the absolute satisfaction He offers: "I am the bread of life. He who comes to me will never go hungry, and he who believes in me will never be thirsty" (John 6:35). Never go hungry! Never thirst!

While it is hard to grasp all of what Jesus meant when He called Himself the "bread of life," here is the important point: The people wanted *stuff*, but Jesus wanted to give them *Himself*. He wanted His hearers to recognize that the supreme hunger of life could only be filled by Him.

Let me offer two thoughts about what it means when Jesus offers us Himself.

Bread of Life Thought #1: In offering us Himself, Jesus promises us a satisfaction unlike anything else in life. Think back to those needs we just listed. Some of our pursuits may meet some of our hungers. Education may bring knowledge. Romance may bring a sense of belonging. Accomplishments may bring significance. Wealth brings some things within reach. The message of Jesus says that no one thing will meet *all* of these hungers.

When we eat, we hunger again. That's obvious, whether we are eating bread or burgers or pizza. What is less obvious is that the other things in life that we think will fill us up sooner or later leave us hungry as well. Christ warns that meeting our physical needs won't meet all the depths of our hunger. Doing more activities can't help us reach everything we aspire to be.

And here's a deep thought to use as a filter on how we spend our lives: Jesus is the measure of anything we think will satisfy us. Until we have fed on the bread of life that Jesus offers, we can't know whether the way we fulfill those other legitimate needs is good or bad.

Not only do we remain unfulfilled when we pursue these hungers, but the more we pursue them the more mixed up we become in understanding where real satisfaction comes from. We are stuck like Andy Harris on Mount Everest, starved for oxygen yet unable to feed our spiritual understanding.

If Jesus were standing right in front of us, He would say, "Don't waste your whole lives scrounging for 'bread.' I don't merely offer you bread. I *am* the bread. I don't merely give you stuff. I give you *Myself*."

Bread of Life Thought #2: In offering us Himself, Jesus is unlike any religious leader in the world. At the heart of every major religion is a leader. Yet there is always a distinction between the person and the teaching. Mohammed is different from the Koran. Buddha didn't claim to be the Noble Path.

Whatever we think of their claims, one reality is undeniable. These men are teachers who point to their teaching or reveal a particular way. It is not Buddha who delivers you; it is his

> Jesus promises us a satisfaction unlike anything else in life. In offering us Himself, Jesus is unlike any religious leader in the world.

"Noble Truths" that instruct you. It is not Mohammed who transforms you; it is the beauty of the Koran that woos you.

By contrast, Jesus didn't just teach or expound His message. *He was identical with His message.* "In Christ," say the Scriptures, "all the fullness of the Deity lives in bodily form" (Col. 2:9). He didn't just proclaim the truth. He said, "I *am* the Truth." He did not just show a way. He said, "I *am* the Way." He did not just open up vistas. He said, "I *am* the door." "I *am*

What Can We Expect of God?

People accuse Christians not only of ruining everyone's fun but even of denying legitimate human needs. The Christian faith doesn't say it is wrong to want things. It doesn't label all needs and desires as "unspiritual."

The hungers of our bodies drive us to meet needs, and God's point isn't that you don't have or shouldn't meet those needs. Jesus fed the hungry. He healed the sick. He transformed water at the wedding when the wine ran out. Jesus just wants you to know that you can be physically, emotionally, socially, or financially full and yet be spiritually empty.

The Bible does promise that "God will meet all your needs according to his glorious riches in Christ Jesus" (Phil. 4:19), and as people point out, "all your needs" means "all your needs." That said, many of us could grow greatly if we obsessed less about what we sometimes label "needs." Take time to think how these Scriptures apply to your life:

- "Man does not live on bread alone, but on every word that comes from the mouth of God" (Matt. 4:4).
- "Seek first [God's] kingdom and his righteousness, and all these things will be given to you as well" (Matt. 6:33).
- "I have learned to be content whatever the circumstances. I know what it is to be in need, and I know what it is to have plenty. I have learned the secret of being content in any and every situation, whether well fed or hungry, whether living in plenty or in want" (Phil. 4:11–12).

the good shepherd" (John 10:11). "I *am* the resurrection and the life" (John 11:25). "I *am* the light of the world" (John 8:12).

Jesus is completely unique in these claims.

What You Get in Buddhism

What Jesus promised as the "reward" of Christianity is that we will enjoy an intimate relationship with the King of the universe. No one will deny the uniqueness of that teaching. Nothing in any other religion even comes close to Christ's claim to be the bread that will fill you up forever.

Take Buddhism, for example, a system of belief rapidly gaining a following in Hollywood, among other places. It's often

> **In Buddhism, you get rules of conduct endlessly multiplied.**

defined as a simple religion of compassion and ethics. The truth is that there is probably no system of belief more complex than Buddhism.

Buddhism starts off with the four noble truths on suffering and then moves to the eightfold path on how to end suffering. So far, so good—very straightforward. But as a devotee enters the eightfold path, there emerge hundreds upon hundreds of other rules to deal with all the circumstances that life presents.

From a simple base of four offenses that determine a Buddhist's status as a true disciple is built an incredible maze of ways to restoration:

- Those who follow Buddha's teachings are given thirty rules on how to ward off pitfalls.

- But before those rules pertain, there are ninety-two rules that apply to just one of the offenses.

- There are seventy-five rules for people becoming Buddhist monks.

- There are 227 rules of discipline to apply for men, 311 for women.

Buddha, by the way, had to be persuaded even to permit women the status of "disciple." After much pleading and cajoling by one of his disciples, he finally gave in to the request, but he laid down extra rules for women.

In a nontheistic system like Buddhism—a system without a personal God or gods foundational to its teachings—ethics become central. The system focuses on decisions of right and wrong, and rules pile up endlessly. The most common prayer for forgiveness in Buddhism, from the Buddhist Common Prayer, reflects this numerical maze:

> I beg leave! I beg leave, I beg leave. . . . May I be freed at all times from the four states of Woe, the Three Scourges, the Eight Wrong Circumstances, the Five Enemies, the Four Deficiencies, the Five Misfortunes, and quickly attain the Path, the Fruition, and the Noble Law of Nirvana, Lord.[3]

Teaching points out the value of morality, but it can't in itself make us moral. It's like a mirror. It can show you if your face is dirty, but the mirror won't wash your face. Buddhism is several steps beyond complicated.

In Christianity, you get Jesus. In Buddhism, you get rules of conduct endlessly multiplied.

What You Get in Hinduism

Hinduism at its heart teaches us that we are to seek union with the divine. Why? Because the Hindu claims that the whole universe is divine and that we are part and parcel of it. In Hinduism, the goal of the individual is to grow past our ignorance and delusions by discovering our divinity and living it out.

The popular Hindu author Deepak Chopra writes this about our purpose of life: "In reality, we are divinity in disguise, and the gods and goddesses in embryo that are contained within us seek to be fully materialized. True success is therefore the experience of the miraculous. It is the unfolding of the divinity within us."[4] Chopra also says, "We must find out for ourselves that inside us is a god or goddess in embryo that wants to be born so that we can express our divinity."[5]

> In Hinduism, you—a forgetful god—obtain union with the impersonal divine universe.

When I read those quotes I can't resist rattling off some questions. Who is the we? Who is the god? Who is the self? Are these different entities that live together inside of us? Is there a god who needs me—*but which me?*—to bring him—*which him if it is actually me?*—to birth so that my deluded self will cease to be deluded and will emerge divine as the real Self? How did god end up in embryonic form in me while I became full grown—so that I will give him the privilege of birth and lose my humanity to find my divinity?

At the risk of being frivolous, if you have ever heard the Abbott and Costello comedy routine "Who's on first?" you can spot this as the ultimate religious version of that frustratingly funny dialogue.

Toward the end of his book, Chopra asks us to make a commitment to these Hindu beliefs. Ask yourself if you can honestly find this believable:

Today I will lovingly nurture the god or goddess in embryo that lies deep within my soul. I will pay attention to the spirit within me that animates both my body and my mind. I will awaken myself to this deep stillness within my heart. I will carry the consciousness of timeless, eternal Being in the midst of time-bound experience.[6]

This is the heart of Hinduism as a belief system—that you and I are gods. One of India's premier philosophers stated as plainly as possibly, "Man is God in a temporary state of self-forgetfulness."

Yet is this reality? Is this what you think when you look in the mirror? Is this what a few thousand years of human history has taught us—that you and I are lonely and confused gods who have lost our way?

Let me offer three thoughts:

- Union with the impersonal force won't ever satisfy our human ache for intimacy—to know and to be known.

- Hinduism offers no clear path for living because believing we are one with an impersonal force defies how we think, how we talk, and how we experience life. Some of the most respected Hindu thinkers have labeled Hinduism as one of the most contradictory systems of life's purpose ever espoused.[7]

- Hinduism couldn't survive the emptiness of calling ourselves gods. Most people know they are anything *but* god—and so gods erupted by the millions, and Hindu temples are crowded with people seeking to worship them.

In Christianity, you get Jesus. In Hinduism, you—a forgetful god—obtain union with the impersonal divine universe.

What You Get in Islam

While Hinduism goes to one extreme—making self god—Islam is at the other extreme. In Islam, the distance between God and humanity is so vast that even those most devoted to Allah never get close to him. Because this distance between Allah and his followers is impossible to cross, worship becomes an incredible clutter of activity designed to bring the worshiper closer. Repetition and submission take the place of a warm relationship.

With all the rituals and rules that a Muslim observes, he never has a certainty that he will go to heaven. A person's destiny is all in the "will of God," they say. A person's destiny is left at the mercy of an unknown will.

Relationship is swallowed up by rules and the real threat of punishment.

One day a Muslim friend and I were out for the day together. I had forgotten that the Ramadan had just begun and suggested that we step into a restaurant for a cup of coffee. Since eating is forbidden during this holy month of daytime fasting, my friend shuddered. "I will spend years in jail for that cup of coffee," he said, so of course I apologized for my suggestion. Then in low tones he admitted that he only practiced his

> **In Islam, you find not closeness to God but worship built on repetition and submission.**

fast in public, and that he still ate in private. "I cannot work ten hours a day without eating," he said. There was an awkward silence, and he muttered these words: "I don't think God is the enforcer of these rules."

Muslims will admit with a smile that during the month of Ramadan more food is sold than during any other month of the year. But its consumption takes place from dusk to dawn rather than from dawn to dusk.

In Christianity, you get Jesus. In Islam, you find not closeness to God but worship built on repetition and submission.

What Makes Eastern Religions So Attractive?

You might read these descriptions of Eastern religions and say, "Well, who wants *that?*" Even so, I think young people face real temptations to join religions such as Buddhism, Hinduism, or Islam. Here is what youth find appealing:

- Buying into another religion relieves them from accusations or feelings of intolerance and exclusivity. They don't have to make a case for Jesus as the one way to God.

- Eastern religions make it possible for young people to be religious without having an absolute God to answer to. They can see God as a deity who doesn't put a fence around them but allows them to roam free, without boundaries on their passions and desires. Specifically, reincarnation lets them make mistakes and enjoy life.

- Eastern religions give an appearance of freedom from doctrine and dogma.

- Islam is appealing because it weds religious fervor with social relief and politics, providing a chance to fight for causes.

- Eastern religions are much more in tune with popular media and the arts.

- Choosing another religion gives a tremendous breadth of individuality while also bringing community—both things youth want. What is overlooked, however, is that Eastern belief systems are all about the destruction of individuality.

The Reality of What God Wants to Give You

The disciples never expected to hear what they did from Jesus. They came to Him wanting bread to fill their stomachs. They discovered that there was bread of a different kind prepared for them and that they had a deeper emptiness than they had imagined.

They had bought their lunch at a nearby restaurant, but they were being invited to a different table. If they continued to eat their own bread, they would soon be hungry again. Jesus was offering them eternal fulfillment with moment-by-moment freshness.

But does "feeding on Jesus" sound so spiritual you think it is a useless way to frame real life? Do you wonder what possessing Jesus as your "bread of life" looks like?

John 4 provides an awe-striking picture of how Jesus deals with each one of us when we are open to His feeding. Jesus had met someone at a well—someone who was a woman, a foreigner, and a sexual sinner. In Israel's culture, those were three reasons Jesus should hate her.

Yet Jesus talked with her. He convinced her that He was kind, and He explained that He was "living water." He told her, "Whoever drinks the water I give him will never thirst. Indeed, the water I give him will become in him a spring of water welling up to eternal life" (v. 14). The transaction was fascinating:

- She had come with a bucket. He sent her back with a spring of living water.

- She had come as a reject. He sent her back being accepted by God Himself.

- She came wounded. He sent her back whole.

- She came full of questions. He sent her back as a source for answers.

- She came living a life of quiet desperation. She ran back overflowing with hope.

The disciples missed it all. They were wandering around looking for lunch.

These are the things that happen when we feed on Jesus. Are you hungry for that? Jesus reminds us that all the "bread" in the world can't satisfy us forever. He is the bread of life that eternally sustains. And He nourishes us like no other has ever done.

FIVE

IS GOD RESPONSIBLE FOR MY PAIN?

Bye, Matt." Matthew's father, suitcase in hand, was headed for the door.

Matthew was on the verge of annihilating a fleet of galactic invaders, and he barely looked up from his video game. "Bye, Dad. See ya."

When Matthew's father traveled on business, he was rarely gone more than two or three days. The trips were so routine that good-byes were no big deal. But when five days had passed, Matthew asked his mother when his father was coming home.

Matthew's mother started to cry. "Matt, your father isn't on a business trip," was all she could stutter. His mother tried to explain what had happened. What Matthew pieced together was that his father had packed his suitcase and gone to live with a girlfriend.

Contact with his father has been scarce since that day. And ever since his father left, Matthew has been full of questions: *What if I had figured out what was going on? What if I had paid more attention when he left? What if I had stood in front of the door? What if I had acted better and helped out more around the house? Why is Dad doing this?*

And Matthew asked himself a truly important question: *Why hasn't God done something to fix this mess?*

Finding Answers to Pain

When suffering strikes our lives, we can't help but ask, "What does God have to do with my pain?" Why does He allow it? If God is good, maybe He isn't *powerful* enough to solve our problems. Or if He is powerful, maybe He isn't *good* enough to help.

Almost every writer who looks at the problem of pain has one thing in common with all others. Each begins with a catalog of horrors and atrocities of unimaginable proportions. It isn't just the destruction of one family. It isn't just one person born blind—like the man in this chapter who met Jesus. It isn't just one baby tragically ill. The list of evil circumstances in the world seems endless.

We don't have a hard time thinking of evils we wish didn't exist. And we can probably agree about three facts:

- *Everyone experiences evil.* The sense of evil is universal across time and culture. Buddha's entire pilgrimage toward "Enlightenment," for example, began because he was absorbed with the mystery of evil and suffering. He was set on his course because of the fact that none of us escapes suffering forever.

- *Evil raises two questions.* We want to know what pain says about *God*—or whatever ultimate force we believe guides the universe. We ask, "Is God the author of pain?" We also want to know what pain says about *us.* We ask, "Is my pain somehow my fault?"

- *Evil has no instant answers.* Any person trying to make sense of a world full of good but convulsing with evil sees this is a complex problem with no easy solution. After centuries of debate, finding an adequate response is still a hard job.

While some people see all the bad happenings of life as things that a cruel God lets slip by without solving, I am convinced that there is no better answer to the problem of suffering and evil than the one offered by the Christian faith.

A Man Born Blind

Jesus faced the question of evil head-on in John 9, on the heels of one of the longest reports of any miracle He performed. A debate raged both before and after this particular healing—and all because everyone in the story wants an explanation for a man's blindness.

As Jesus was walking with His disciples, a blind man crossed their path. The disciples didn't merely want to witness the miracle of sight restored. They wanted to know God's role in this tragic situation. Here is what comes next:

> As he went along, he saw a man blind from birth. His disciples asked him, "Rabbi, who sinned, this man or his parents, that he was born blind?"
>
> "Neither this man nor his parents sinned," said Jesus, "but this happened so that the work of God might be displayed in his life. As long as it is day, we must do the work of him who sent me. Night is coming, when no one can work. While I am in the world, I am the light of the world."
>
> Having said this, he spit on the ground, made some mud with the saliva, and put it on the man's eyes. "Go," he told him, "wash in the Pool of Siloam" (this word means Sent). So the man went and washed, and came home seeing.

His neighbors and those who had formerly seen him begging asked, "Isn't this the same man who used to sit and beg?" Some claimed that he was.

Others said, "No, he only looks like him."

But he himself insisted, "I am the man."

"How then were your eyes opened?" they demanded.

He replied, "The man they call Jesus made some mud and put it on my eyes. He told me to go to Siloam and wash. So I went and washed, and then I could see." (John 9:1–11)

The arguments surrounding this healing are long and fascinating. In verses 13 through 33, the Jewish leaders debate the question we looked at in chapter 2—where Jesus comes from. As the scene closes, we see the blind man worshiping Jesus, an action that is due God alone (v. 38).

And notice the question that set up the scene. One of the disciples abruptly asked Jesus, "Who sinned, this man or his parents, that he was born blind?" In other words, "Is this man to blame for his plight, or is someone else?" And in a yet wider view, "Is God responsible for our pain?"

Jesus shocked them with His response. The young man wasn't responsible. Nor were his parents. "This happened," Jesus said, "so that the work of God might be displayed in his life."

Answers, Anyone?

Let's remember that *every* world-view—not just Christianity— must explain evil and suffering. As we search for an answer to the problem of evil, we wind up in one of three spots:

- Possibility 1: Evil unmistakably proves that God doesn't exist, as atheists say.

- Possibility 2: Evil isn't really real, as Hindus and some atheists claim.

- Possibility 3: Evil is explained by the Christian view of God and His purposes.

It's not enough just to raise doubts. It's not adequate for a challenger to Christianity to dislike the answer the Bible provides without offering a better answer.

Real Answers for Real People

I want to say something up front. Wherever I travel, I run into people in pain. I know that when I teach a group of people that *someone* present is in an episode of heart-crushing suffering. As you read this book, that person might be you . . . or a friend . . . or a family member. I want you to think about these very real people in very real pain and notice two things.

First, trying only to answer the *intellectual struggles* of pain is heartless. If you break your arm in phys ed class and your shoulder has come out of its socket, you don't run to your biology teacher for a lecture on the calcium content of bone. If your parents are hurtling toward divorce, you don't want a discussion on the biblical responsibilities of a man and woman in marriage. When you witness person-to-person cruelty and someone tries to explain the sociological implications of violence to you, you may get angry. Who wants logic when your heart is broken?

Second, yet trying only to soothe *emotional wounds* is brainless. Dealing only with *feelings* while our minds churn with questions won't bring healing. When pain strikes, our short-term need is for sympathy. We want comfort. We want a painkiller. But long-term healing of hurt feelings seldom happens without making sense of pain.

How Can I Reach My Hurting Friends?

Hurting people are all around you. What's the best way to help? Whether you are comforting a friend crying on your shoulder, debating questions of good and evil, or trying to help a classmate find God, you need to do the following:

- *Ask questions and listen hard to the answers.* The most important task you have is to see people in context. Suppose a seventeen-year-old, when she was fourteen, saw her father die in a tragic car accident. You need to understand that background, because you need to address not just *what* a person believes but why she believes it. Many atheists shake their fists at God because of tragedies they have experienced firsthand and full-force. They will brush aside any answers from you that don't acknowledge the reality of their pain.
- Find "points of entry" that are meaningful for your friends. Preaching a sermon or doing anything that looks like Bible thumping might be a very unacceptable starting point to talk. But a friend might be receptive to a note or a good piece of music. Sometimes you can best reach a person if what you have to say about Jesus is a sidelight to what is going on. Try to talk while you are driving or watching baseball— something that doesn't feel like a frontal assault.
- Never underestimate the value of your life. As you try to help people with problems or even introduce them to Jesus, you truly might not see any results right now. But what you do now will bear fruit later. Countless people tell me, "There was this girl I knew back in college. I used to laugh at her, but now I

know she had life figured out." Your life will bring long-term returns.

- Avoid the appearance of winning an argument. You can respond effectively to any question without the challenger feeling crushed. The most important thing to know when you have clinched an argument is how to back off, so you don't rub someone's nose in the dirt. If you go too far, you provoke an angry defense. You want people to think, "He respected what I said, and yet I think what he says makes more sense."

Whether you are tending hurts of your own or the hurts of someone else, your explanation must meet both the intellectual and the emotional demands of the question. I believe that the biblical world-view is the only one that

- accepts the reality of evil and suffering,
- explains both the cause and the purpose, and
- offers God-given strength to survive it.

Those who refuse to accept the truths that Jesus teaches will find that pain continues to get in the way of grasping God.

The Atheist's Dodge

Atheism employs the existence of evil as one of its main challenges to Christianity. Try hard to track this argument, because you are bound to hear it as you hike through school. And you are bound to find people at various spots on this trail of illogic.

Atheists argue that because evil exists, God does not. Atheists say that the reality of evil proves that God isn't real. If real,

God, after all, would solve all the world's problems.

Christianity immediately confronts that idea. The argument goes like this:

- If evil exists, then we have to assume that good exists—or we wouldn't know the difference.

- If good exists, we have to assume that a moral law exists— or we would have no way to measure good and evil.

- If a moral law exists, we have to say that there is a moral lawgiver—or we would have no basis for an objective moral law.

By an "objective moral law," I mean a definition of good and evil that is absolutely true—true at all times and all places for all people—whether we believe it or not.

Christians have long argued that the design we see all around us shows that the world was fashioned by a Designer. The belief that someone made what we see is like a reasonable explanation of reality based on a clear case of cause and effect.

We live in a world, after all, where any effect can be traced back to a cause. An example: If you pull the family car into your driveway and your parents see a broken taillight and crumpled rear fender, you would be foolish to tell your parents, "It just happened." Maybe you backed into something. Maybe someone ran into you. But something made the dent. Something *caused* the effect.

Over the years, naturalists—people who believe nothing exists in the universe besides matter, including God—have tried to do away with this highly reasonable reasoning.

- First they denied *cause and effect* as a proof of God's existence. Why do we have to have a cause? Why can't the universe just be?

- Then they denied *design* as an argument for God's existence. Why do we need a Designer? Why couldn't the world all have just jumbled together with the appearance of design?

- Now they deny *morality* as an argument for God's existence. Why do we need God to explain our perception of right and wrong? Why can't the moral sense of humans just be a pragmatic reality?

Arguing that evil is real actually creates two huge problems for atheists: (1) it implies the existence of a moral lawgiver, and (2) it means there are moral absolutes they are obligated to follow.

And *something* has to have caused humanity to know right from wrong, since we would have to discard our whole human experience to do away with cause and effect. We would be accepting the moral equivalent of the belief that car fenders dent themselves. Since something has to explain our moral sense, atheists come up with another explanation.

> An "objective moral law" is a definition of good and evil that is absolutely true—true at all times and all places for all people—whether we believe it or not.

Atheists argue that evolution is the cause of our moral sense. When atheists admit that humans have a sense of right and wrong, they need a cause for that fact other than God. Not surprisingly, they say that evolution caused our moral sense. Now for someone who denies the existence of God but accepts the presence of evil, this argument is very compelling. When a Christian says that only God could give people a sense of right and wrong, the skeptic usually has an answer ready. "Who needs God? Why can't evolution explain our moral sense?"

Again, however, there are holes in the atheist's argument. Here are two:

- First, it's fascinating that atheists want a *cause* for suffering or a *design* for suffering, but they have already denied that either of these are necessary to account for the effects we see every day.

- Second, no evolutionist has explained how an impersonal, amoral, "it-just-happened" beginning of the universe—combined with the amoral process of evolution—has produced a moral basis of life.

Doesn't it seem odd that of all the billions of permutations and combinations that a random universe could produce that we would end up with ideas of the true, the good, and the beautiful? In fact, why call anything good and evil? Why not call them orange and purple? That way, we settle from the start that what we perceive to be good and evil are merely different preferences, one as good as the other. (By the way, Bertrand Russell tried that approach and looked quite pathetic at it.)

The claim that evolution produced our moral sense must not feel like solid footing even to some atheists, because some try a final, desperate maneuver.

Some atheists argue that evil doesn't really exist. Listen to this far-fetched explanation by one of atheism's champions, Richard Dawkins of Oxford. Sooner or later at school you will hear about Dawkins, a brilliant scientist whose books sell far and wide. His eloquence, however, can mask the absurdity of his arguments.

In a universe of blind physical forces and genetic replication some people are going to get hurt, other people are going to get lucky, and you won't find any rhyme or reason in it, nor any justice. The universe we observe has precisely the properties we should expect if there is, at the bottom, no design, no purpose, no evil and no other good. Nothing but blind pitiless indifference. DNA neither knows nor cares. DNA just is. And we dance to its music.[1]

Do you see what has happened? The skeptic started with a long list of life's most horrible things, saying, "These are immoral; therefore, there is no God." But evolutionists can't afford to raise these problems, since their own system has no way to create the sense of right and wrong that almost all of us recognize. So what then does the skeptic do? Some conclude that there really isn't such a thing as evil after all.

> **Could you tell a rape victim that her rapist merely danced to his DNA?**

The next time you show up in science class with your homework unfinished, tell your teacher that Richard Dawkins said you could dance to your DNA.

Actually, don't.

Let's see how well Dawkins's theory works to explain the horrors of life. Could you tell a rape victim that her rapist merely danced to his DNA? Would it make sense to the victims of Auschwitz that their tormentors were fulfilling their genetic destiny? And would the loved ones of those cannibalized by Jeffrey Dahmer accept that he was merely drunk on his genetic juices?

In lectures to the British Humanist Association in 1992, Dawkins made another astounding assertion. Having debunked the idea of God and explained away evil as DNA's dance, he tackles another problem: How should we explain, then, the sense of morality that we find in the human experience? Why do we even ask questions about good and evil? Dawkins has the answer—viruses. A virus scrambles the data within the human gene and spits out this misinformation. If we could somehow delete the virus that led us to think this way, we would be stripped clean of these irritating ideas of God, good, and evil.[2]

In Dawkins-speak, those who asked Jesus what caused a blind man's loss of sight needed an antivirus program. In fact, Jesus Himself would need to be scanned with up-to-date virus definitions. And, I suppose, anyone who complains about the Holocaust needs to be quarantined and his blood sample mailed off to the antivirus research labs.

Let's not forget that Dawkins is, of course, free from the virus and can therefore provide us with correct moral programming. More seriously, let's not forget that we have circled back to the beginning of the atheist's argument—and if evil is denied, then how can evil be said to disprove God's existence?

Slicing Up Baby

I put Dawkins's theory to the test with some students at Oxford University. I asked a group of skeptics, "If I took a baby and sliced it to pieces before you, would I have done anything wrong?" They had just denied that objective moral values exist. At my question there was silence—and then the lead voice in the group said, "I would not like it, but no, I could not say you have done anything wrong."

My! What sensitivity! He would not like it. My! What irrationality. He could not brand it wrong.

But would he think it wrong if I carved *him* up?

All we have to do to prove that objective moral values exist is to push to the extreme, and suddenly we find that yes, all reasonable people will declare that they are absolutely sure there are indeed behaviors that are absolutely wrong. And if these objective moral values exist, the best explanation is that God exists, because the best answer of the atheist—evolution—can't produce these values.

How would other religions answer the question behind the disciples' question: Is God cruelly responsible for evil?

Hinduism's Answer to Evil

Hinduism has no shortage of extensive answers, but sometimes those answers are terribly confusing. And on this topic, the difficulty with Hinduism is that it has no single all-encompassing response to the problem of suffering. Nevertheless, there are undeniable problems with the obvious answers that emerge from Hindu belief.

For example, by declaring everything in the physical world to be non-real, illusory, changing, and transitory, Hinduism has to deny what the rest of us accept as reality.

Here's what I mean by denying reality. A humorous story is told of India's leading philosopher, Shankara. He had just finished lecturing the king on the deception of the mind and its delusion of material reality. The next day, the king let loose an elephant that went on a rampage, and Shankara ran up a tree to find safety. When the king asked him why he ran if the elephant was non-real, Shankara, not to be outdone, said, "What the king actually saw was a non-real me climbing up a non-real tree!"

One might add, "That is a non-real answer."

While the story of Shankara is a fable, there is no way for classical Hinduism to deal with the problem of evil. To deny that evil is real doesn't diminish wickedness nor does it satisfy the heart's desire to seek purity. That is why so much of Hindu worship is steeped in purification rites and why all of popular

Does the Bible Teach Reincarnation?

Reincarnation is a central, nonnegotiable part of Hindu philosophy. Reincarnation claims we exist in a recurring cycle in which the life we live now determines our lot in a next life.

Instead of saying what I think reincarnation in Hinduism means, listen instead to the words of the Hindu scriptures:

> Accordingly, those who are of pleasant conduct here— the prospect is, indeed, that they will enter a pleasant womb, either the womb of a Brahman [the priestly class], or the womb of a Kshatriya [the professional or warrior class], or the womb of a Vaisya [the working class]. But those who are of stinking conduct here— the prospect is, indeed, that they will enter a stinking womb of a dog, or the womb of a swine, or the womb of an outcast. (Chandogya Upanishad, 5.10.8)

This jolting passage says that what we do in this life will be paid back as we live out our next life in vegetable, animal, or human form.

This clearly isn't the teaching of Scripture. In the story of the man born blind, Jesus stated that there was no connection between a previous act and the man's current condition. Even in the disciples' question, there is no mention of "previous" lives. And the rest of Scripture simply allows no possibility of the actions in this life impacting some future life. It teaches that humans die once and then face judgment (Heb. 9:27).

Hinduism is filled with forms of worship, fear of punishment, means of obtaining God's favor, and so on.

Hinduism also ends up with philosophical problems beyond measure. We have to ask what has brought on this "illusion" of evil if everything is part of the divine reality. Hinduism explains that this perception of evil is the result of ignorance, but that only pushes the question one step further. If all is One, and evil is an illusion born out of ignorance, then who is the source of the ignorance but the One? And if the One is the source of the ignorance, then the One lacks true knowledge. And if the One lacks true knowledge, then the One is not true God.

But Hinduism's real answer to the question of the man who was blind from birth is reincarnation. In fact, some Eastern thinkers have jumped on the blind man's encounter with Jesus as proof that the Bible teaches reincarnation. How else could the man have sinned before birth? Their view, though, is both a misrepresentation of the passage and a failure to face up to what their doctrine of reincarnation actually teaches.

Buddhism's Answer to Evil

If a bully chased you down after school and not only stole your book bag but left you bloodied and beaten, strict Hindu philosophy would say that the attack was an illusion. How would Buddhism respond? It would say you got what you had coming.

Actually, both Hinduism and Buddhism invoke the doctrine of reincarnation to explain the problem of pain. The opening lines of the Buddhist scriptures say that every individual is the sum total of what he or she thought in his or her past life.

So, for Buddhism, too, the answer to the disciples' question regarding the blind man's predicament—"Who sinned, this man or his parents?"—would be, "Both this man and his parents have sinned." The suffering of the blind man is the inheritance of his past life's sin, and it is the lot of the parents to inherit this situation.

The incredible aspect of this teaching is that the more painful a person's existence, the more certain it is that the previous life is successfully paying its dues—so that when one picks up the body of a little child deformed from birth, what Buddhists call *kamma* is in operation. The pain of this present life is paying for the sins of a past life.

In striking contrast, the Christian message recognizes the horror of evil and seeks to offer a better reason for God to allow suffering. Let's turn to the Christian response to see the difference.

A Christian View of Suffering

When we pull together all that Scripture has said about pain and suffering, we find six elements that combine to explain evil in a way that satisfies both our minds and emotions. What Christianity offers isn't a quick answer but one that

- accepts the reality of evil and suffering,
- explains both the cause and the purpose, and
- offers God-given strength to survive it.

Let's take a closer look at these six facts about suffering.

Fact #1: God's goodness is beyond comparison. The God of the Bible reveals Himself as the author of life and as a Being who is good beyond comparison. In fact, God isn't merely good; God is holy.

If we sat down with pencil and paper and tried to describe our "ideal God," we could come up with an interesting list. But our list would only be accurate to the extent that it reflects what God has shown us of Himself.

- *God is perfect beyond our wildest imagination.* What this means is that as human beings we are never in a position to draw up qualifications for God to meet in order for us to call Him good. Instead, God's flawless character is the measure of us and our definitions of good. This difference is what makes the Christian understanding of good and evil almost impossible for a skeptic to grasp.

- *Even at our best we fall short of God's magnificence.* You might know the familiar Bible verse Romans 3:23, that "all have sinned and fall short of the glory of God." But here's a picture: The Old Testament prophet Isaiah was awestruck when God revealed Himself to him. Isaiah was a morally good man, but he immediately sensed that he was unfit to be in God's presence. He fell on his face. He hadn't stepped into the living room of someone slightly *better* than him. He was in the throne room of the One who is *infinitely perfect* (Isa. 6:1–8).

- *The holiness of God is like light in a dark world.* Just as sunrise exposes the thoughts and deeds of the night and often leaves a hungover feeling of wrong, God's holiness shines in our lives to expose evil. For anyone who loves God, though, the light of God is also a welcome guide and a healing presence (John 3:19–21; Isa. 60:1–3).

Whatever confusion we have about good and evil, we find the answer in Him.

Fact #2: This holy God has a plan for life. God declares, "I make known the end from the beginning, from ancient times, what is still to come. I say: My purpose will stand, and I will do all that I please" (Isa. 46:10). He says, "All the days ordained for me were written in your book before one of them came to be" (Ps. 139:16).

God has a plan both for the world and for each of us as individuals. We are not, as philosopher Jean-Paul Sartre said, empty bubbles floating on the sea of nothingness. We aren't on a cruise lacking purpose or destination or instruments. We are going places!

The blind man, the disciples, and the neighbors—they all knew the Bible's big story. In the beginning God had created the heavens and the earth. God was in control over the circumstances of every life. But how did this man's blindness fit into the story?

We must understand whatever happens to us against the larger story of God's purpose for our lives. Someday we will fully grasp that larger plot, and suddenly our subplots will make sense. But for now, for as long as we can't understand what we suffer, we don't have to groan that our situation is an unsolvable mystery. What we *can* know is that God's purposes work for a higher good—a good even higher, in the case of the blind man, than God's wondrous gift of sight. God's purpose for our lives is that we grasp His glory.

When we suffer, we can be sure it has a place in God's larger scheme.

Fact #3: God's plan is that we experience a love powered by His own love and practiced within His prescribed boundaries. Think of what love looks like apart from God. Millions of lives are hurt every day in the name of love, including a few lives probably devastated at your school today by nasty breakup notes delivered to lockers. Love might make the world go 'round, but the wrong kind of love spins us sick.

Love is at the heart of God's big plan for us and our world. God's intent is that we experience His love—a *sacred* love. Experiencing His love is how we have the right kind of love to pass on to others (1 John 4:19).

What does all this have to do with suffering? Everything. You see, when skeptics claim that a good God would have made us to choose only good, they completely miss what goodness is in God's eyes. Goodness involves a choice. It's a life willingly and totally lived for God even when that choice is hard and costly. It's a love *from* God and *for* God that carries us through life's hardest battles.

We make a deadly mistake when we think that a love apart from God is all we need to carry us through life's hardships.

Fact #4: The death of Jesus on the cross shows the reality of evil—and God's solution for it. Jesus' death on the cross is the only way that we can admit the reality of evil without charging God with ignoring evil. The core of the Christian message displays a wholly unique expression in the face of evil. Jesus' death pounds home a message with triple-force. It demonstrates

- the destructiveness of evil, which is the cause of suffering,

- the ability to withstand undeserved suffering, and

- the plan of God to put an end to suffering.

Nobel Peace Prize winner Elie Wiesel relates in one of his essays an experience he had when he was a prisoner in Auschwitz. A Jewish prisoner was being executed while the rest of the prisoners were forced to watch. As the Jewish prisoner hung on the gallows—kicking and struggling in the throes of death, refusing to die—an onlooker was heard to mutter under his breath with increasing desperation, "Where is God? Where is He?"

From out of nowhere, Wiesel says, a voice within him spoke to his own heart, saying, "Right there on the gallows; where else?"[3]

When we suffer, God suffers with us. Jesus suffered the full brunt of undeserved pain. Jesus had done nothing wrong, yet He was nailed to a cross. If anyone had reason to cry "Foul!" and demand relief from suffering, it was Jesus. And yet Jesus stayed on the cross to destroy sin and death for any who would trust in Him.

When we suffer, we can be sure God is closer than we can fathom. When we suffer, we can be sure that God understands. And when we suffer, we can be sure that, in Christ, God is working a plan to end evil.

Fact #5: Evil isn't merely someone else's problem. Evil isn't just something *outside* of us that inflicts suffering on *us*. Evil is something *inside* of us that inflicts suffering on *others*.

I remember talking to an incredibly wealthy businessman who repeatedly raised this question: "But what about all the evil in this world?" A friend finally said to him, "I hear you always wanting to see a solution to the problem of evil around you. Are you as troubled by the problem of evil inside you?" In the pin-drop silence that followed, the man's face showed his insincerity. The question isn't what evil says about God; it's what evil says about us.

The longer I have thought about this question of evil, the more convinced I am of the extreme insincerity of many questioners. During one forum on evil and suffering, one atheist asked me, "If you found out that God didn't exist after all, what would you immediately do that you aren't doing now out of fear of Him?"

That tells you a mind-set: "If God would get off my back, I could do many more things." It fails to see that the sinful human heart longs for its own way and isn't thinking about who or what it might trample.

When we see that evil that we ourselves cause, what we suffer at the hands of others often seems trivial.

Fact #6: Pain isn't our deepest problem. Pain can cause despair. But a deeper despair comes from pursuing pleasures other than God.

Suffering causes a huge crisis of faith. It raises questions about God. It prompts questions about ourselves. But here is the truth: It seldom is pain that drives us into emptiness. Meaningless comes from drowning in the oceans of our pleasures. Pleasure gone wrong is a greater curse than physical blindness.

Have you noticed that people who say "My life has no meaning" are rarely ones who suffer real pain? Meaninglessness doesn't come from being weary of pain but from being weary of pleasure.

> The problem of evil has ultimately one source: our rebellion against God's holiness.

Pain often forces us to find God. Pleasure frequently causes us to ignore Him.

This is where Jesus' answer to the question of the blind man comes home with extraordinary power. He said that the man's blindness was due neither to the sin of the man nor of his parents but so that the glory of God might be displayed. God's healing of the blind man's physical sight was marvelous. But the greater cure was that his spiritual eyes were opened to recognize Jesus.

This is no glib answer to evil if spiritual sight is what we really need.

When your life is free from pain, don't allow your life to run free from God.

An End to Evil

Evil is real. But the problem of evil has ultimately one source: our rebellion against God's holiness.

Evil seems mysterious only because we are engulfed in it as people who both suffer and cause suffering. And there is ultimately only one antidote: God's transforming work inside our hearts to bring an end to evil. His work softens us to become part of the solution and not part of the problem. And His work is the victorious assault on evil that Jesus accomplished at the cross.

WON'T JESUS ANSWER EVERY QUESTION?

Soon after the collapse of the Soviet Union, a Russian general invited me to speak at a discussion with seven high-ranking military leaders at the Center for Geopolitical Strategy in Moscow. The atmosphere was cold and antagonistic, and the expressions on their faces were hard. One by one, they launched attacks on religion in general—and on Christianity in particular. I tried to defuse one question after another, but I could tell the discussion was going nowhere. They kept backtracking to what they saw as Christendom's bloody history.

One officer, with great antagonism in his voice, leaned toward me and said, "As a child I remember seeing a German soldier come into my home and shoot my grandmother to death. On his belt buckle were the words 'God is for us.' *That* is what religion has done for our country!"

He was right.

Perhaps he didn't remember or even know that the Nazis hadn't carved God's name on those buckles. The buckles were leftovers from previous German governments, dug out when the Nazi war machine ground down into a serious lack of equipment. But that aside, the symbol of the cross has been so repeatedly stamped on weapons of war that the message of Christ has come to represent power and hatred to many.

I paused and admitted to him that I partially agreed with what he had said. That surprised him, and he cautiously lowered his guard. Then I said, "But you know, General, Jesus never came to establish a government by force. He did not even talk about political systems. He came to rule in the hearts of people, not to establish political power. He asks to live in *you*, not to control your state."

A Different King

I have found that hostile challengers of Christianity come in many forms. One of the most common is the person who assumes that Christ—and Christians, His representatives—came to "shove religion down my throat."

> Jesus' kingdom wasn't the kind to be built by military might, by power, or by force of any kind.

Have you seen these people react with the same caution and cynicism as those generals? You might notice

- a friend whose face hardens when you talk about Jesus,

- teachers who have memorized a long list of atrocities committed in the name of Christianity, such as the Inquisition, the burning of heretics, and the silencing of scientists and others who challenged church teachings,

- a rebellious older sister who thinks her parents are forcing her to accept their faith—and their morals,

- a psychologist who thinks faith makes people puppets, and

- college students who have taken an introductory religion course and now regard Scripture as just another human book full of dos and don'ts—or taken a history class and now see the Bible as the tool of political oppression.

If you aren't sensing these attitudes around you right now, you surely will sniff them out when you enter college or the workplace.

If history has proven anything, it is that the spread of the gospel by the sword or by some other pressure to conform has done nothing but distort Christ and disgrace His message. Despite the assumptions of many people, Jesus' kingdom wasn't the kind to be built by military might, by power, or by force of any kind.

What Jesus wants are willing followers.

The Real Aim of Jesus

We can look at the words of Jesus and the pattern of His life and see that He wanted nothing to do with a religion forced either on individuals or on nations. One of the most profound insights into this fact came from Napoleon (1769–1821), the French emperor and one of the greatest military commanders in all of history. Having conquered all of civilized Europe, Napoleon understood power. Yet he saw that Jesus came with different motives and methods. He offered this extraordinary statement about Jesus Christ:

> Alexander, Caesar, Charlemagne and I myself have founded great empires; but upon what did these creations of our genius depend? Upon force. Jesus alone founded His empire upon love, and to this very day millions will die for Him. . . . I think I understand something of human nature; and I tell you, all

But What If I Didn't Do Any of Those Things?

Sooner or later, every Christian who shares the faith is blasted with the charge that Christianity systematically forces its beliefs on others. The complaint might be that Christianity strips individuals of their freedom by imposing rules about morality. The complaint might also be that Christianity has forced its beliefs and values on whole societies.

It's frustrating to be blamed for the sins of others. It's even more frustrating when blame comes out of the blue. You are better off knowing some of the sins—real and imagined—attributed to your faith. (As you encounter these issues, it's important to study *all* the facts about these actual events. For example, it's important to note that Galileo never stepped outside the bounds of the Bible—and his imprisonment was the unfortunate result of the church's misinterpretation of Scripture. Only as you see situations in their context can you counter the myths that have been handed down for generations.)

- The *Inquisition* was a tool of the medieval church to hunt out heretics, people accused of holding less-than-orthodox beliefs. In 1252, Pope Innocent IV officially sanctioned torture to extract the truth from suspects, and by 1498, more than two thousand people had been burned at the stake in Spain alone.
- Scientists whose discoveries were said to conflict with the Bible were silenced by the church. *Galileo* (1564–1642), for example, was sentenced to per-

manent house arrest for teaching that the earth revolved around the sun.

- Protestants also persecuted those who argued against established beliefs. The government led by John Calvin (1509–64) in Geneva, Switzerland, burned Spanish doctor and theologian Michael Servetus at the stake for contradicting the biblical teaching of the Trinity.

- As a result of the *Salem Witch Trials* (1692), twenty people were executed. The "witch hunt" began after several young girls said they had been taught occult arts by adults in the community.

- Critics have long seen Christianity as a tool of *colonial imperialism* and the cause of exploitation and destruction of native cultures around the world. Even today *missionary efforts* are labeled "ethnocentric," and *missionaries* are accused of political motives, including being fronts for the CIA. The spiritual and social good accomplished by countless missionaries is predictably ignored.

- One of the most common modern illustrations comes from Kosovo, where the Serbs—traditionally members of the Orthodox branch of Christianity—have perpetrated ethnic cleansings of their Albanian neighbors—traditionally Muslims.

While it is difficult to change anyone's mind on these issues, you can raise three issues with those who accuse you of the same types of sins:

- Point to the flawless life of Jesus and His clear rejection of force-fed religion.

- Highlight the difference between the acts of so-called "Christian" nations and political leaders and the acts of true followers of Jesus.
- Even as you boldly share the good news of Jesus, demonstrate through graciousness and respect that you are in no way interested in pushing religion on anyone.

these were men, and I am a man: none else is like Him; Jesus Christ was more than man. . . . I have inspired multitudes with such an enthusiastic devotion that they would have died for me . . . but to do this it was necessary that I should be visibly present with the electric influence of my looks, my words, of my voice. When I saw men and spoke to them, I lighted up the flame of self-devotion in their hearts. . . . Christ alone has succeeded in so raising the mind of man towards the unseen, that it becomes insensible to the barriers of time and space. Across a chasm of eighteen hundred years, Jesus Christ makes a demand which is beyond all others difficult to satisfy; He asks for that which a philosopher may often seek in vain at the hands of his friends, or a father of his children, or a bride of her spouse, or a man of his brother. He asks for the human heart; He will have it entirely to Himself. He demands it unconditionally; and forthwith His demand is granted. Wonderful! In defiance of time and space, the soul of man, with all its powers and faculties, becomes an annexation to the empire of Christ. All who sincerely believe in Him, experience that remarkable, supernatural love towards Him. This phenomenon is unaccountable; it is altogether beyond the scope of man's creative powers. Time, the great destroyer, is powerless to extinguish this sacred flame; time can neither exhaust its

Are Their Questions Their Own?

Doubt is contagious. Disbelief passes from person to person like the latest flu bug, with little resistance raised.

I see this at schools, but I don't blame the students. Behind many doubt-infected students are teachers who don't let students think for themselves.

Once I was lecturing at a university on "Ethics and the Invasion of Cyberspace." I was told that I was invited as the token Christian so at least one speaker would propose an absolute basis for decisions of right and wrong.

After the lecture, we sat down for a lunch hosted by faculty members and student leaders. During the lunch, one of the faculty members said something like this: "All this philosophizing about an objective morality seems so highbrow and philosophically weighty. The basic question I have is simple: How do we keep students from cheating?"

At the end of the lunch, a handful of students surrounded me with a flurry of questions. One of them, in low tones, said, "I really have a problem. I was asked by my professor to come and listen to your lecture and to critique what you said. But the truth is that after hearing your arguments, I agree with you."

"Well, then," I asked, "why don't you say that in your paper?"

"Oh no! I will be definitely docked in my grades if I agree with your reasoning. My professor was sure I would disagree with you and wanted me to shred you. I'm a straight-A student, and I can't afford to drop my grade."

"Are you sure your professor will penalize you just for agreeing with my position?" I asked her.

"Positive," she said.

"Was your professor here at the luncheon?" I asked.

"Yes," came an obviously hesitant response.

"Who was it?"

There was an awkward silence, and then an even more uncomfortable admission. "She was the one who asked you how to keep students from cheating."

So much for the genuine hunger for truth.

strength nor put a limit to its range. This is it, which strikes me most; I have often thought of it. This it is which proves to me quite convincingly the Divinity of Jesus Christ.[1]

These are more than well-phrased words. With unbelievable insight, Napoleon saw how Jesus conquered—not by force but by winning hearts.

The Sounds of Silence

At the trial that led to His crucifixion, Jesus stood before the Roman governor of Israel charged with treason against Caesar. Even though any honest glance at His life would show that Jesus had never come to establish a kingdom by force, that was the accusation nailed to Him.

As Jesus stood before Pontius Pilate and others who accused Him, His actions were fascinating. With a calmness that unnerved His questioners, He stood silent before them. His silence told the whole story, and all of the allegations by critics past and present that Jesus came to "shove religion down our throats" were examined—and exploded—that day.

Jesus' trial did begin with a brief interchange between Jesus and Pilate. The answers He *did* give help us understand the answers He *didn't*.

Pilate's questions were straight to the point of Jesus' political intentions: "Are you the king of the Jews?" and "What is it you have done?" (John 18:33, 35). Jesus replied, "My kingdom is not of this world. If it were, my servants would fight to prevent my arrest by the Jews. But now my kingdom is from another place."

"You are a king, then!" said Pilate.

Jesus answered, "You are right in saying I am a king. In fact, for this reason I was born, and for this I came into the world, to testify to the truth. Everyone on the side of truth listens to me" (vv. 36–37).

> The kingship of Jesus had *nothing* to do with force-fed religion but had *everything* to do with finding willing followers.

Jesus wanted Pilate to understand that His kingship had *nothing* to do with governing a nation or a culture but had *everything* to do with the rule of the heart. It had *nothing* to do with force-fed religion but had *everything* to do with finding willing followers.

The whole life and ministry of Jesus had been His claim. He had made His claim once more. And then, when confronted by truth-hating, contagious doubt, He remained silent.

There are four specific times that Jesus was silent along the trail to His death. Let's look at them.

- *Jesus was silent when the accusations against Him were wrongful and ridiculous.* In Mark 14:60, Jesus was tried before the Sanhedrin, the main judicial council for the Jews. The entire episode before the Sanhedrin was an effort to frame Him. False witnesses gave conflicting testimony.

Truth Tip: When Is It Right to Be Silent?

It would be easy to take Jesus' silence as an excuse never to speak up for your faith. But notice: Jesus only stopped speaking after a lifetime of bold proclamation. He discerned the spiritual condition of His opponents perfectly. And He was deliberately silent so He could lay down His life for us.

How Jesus acted has everything to do with how we share our faith at school, on a team, in a club, at home, or in our neighborhoods.

- Jesus was silent when the accusations against Him were wrongful and ridiculous. When you are emotionally outraged by an insult against you or your faith, take a breather. You can say, "I need to think about what you've said" and wait until you have a better response than blowing up.

- Jesus was silent when minds were already made up. With a teacher, for example, who claims that all life can be explained by evolution, don't offer a counter-argument. Ask a question—and then listen. Ask a leading question like, "What about the cell? How could the cell have developed through evolution?"

- Jesus was silent when people wanted a show. Remember how Herod and his friends made fun of Jesus? A person who stands silently in the face of mocking and hate-filled people is like a spotlight on wrong. Your silence screams the truth of God's character.

- Jesus was silent when His job was done. Unlike Jesus, you are not the eternal judge of people's souls.

You never know exactly what is going on in someone else's head. But you can still ask God to show you how and when to share your faith—and when to be quiet as people process what you have said.

Their charges didn't add up. Yet Jesus remained silent. Why? Their lies were obvious. And when people don't admit the obvious, either truth or truthfulness has died. What Jesus showed was silent goodness in the face of orchestrated evil. Any time evil organizes, its fury is like the breath of hell. Nothing can put out the flame.

- *Jesus was silent when minds were already made up.* When the high priests repeated their charges of Jesus' alleged treason before Pilate, Jesus was silent a second time (Mark 15:5). He knew that His opponents were determined to crucify Him, and any words of self-defense would have been pointless, especially since the priests were backed by a crowd just as uninterested in truth.

- *Jesus was silent when people wanted a show.* Herod and his band of mockers wanted Jesus to do a miracle on command. This was the third time Jesus said nothing. The Bible says this:

> When Herod saw Jesus, he was greatly pleased, because for a long time he had been wanting to see him. From what he had heard about him, he hoped to see him perform some miracle. He plied him with many questions, but Jesus gave him no answer. . . . Then Herod and his soldiers ridiculed and mocked him. Dressing him in an elegant robe, they sent him back to Pilate. That day Herod and Pilate became friends—before this they had been enemies. (Luke 23:8–9, 11–12)

What a terrifying situation! Many people want Jesus to be nothing more than a miracle worker or an entertainer. And how ironic—enemies became friends out of a shared desire to be rid of Him. Has anything changed since then?

- *Jesus was silent when His job was done.* The fourth time Jesus chose to be silent was when Pilate became fearful at Christ's claim to be the Son of God. "Where do you come from?" he asked. But Jesus remained silent (John 19:8). He had already told Pilate where He came from. But Pilate didn't have the courage to deal with His answer.

Pilate and Jesus' accusers had proven they were not really looking for truth. Jesus had spoken. Acted. Performed miracles. He had repeated His message. Absolutely nothing that Jesus could have said would have convinced them of who He really was, or caused them to even care. And now, since they were unwilling to hear, Jesus was unwilling to speak.

Jesus didn't push Himself on anyone. And He wouldn't answer their every last question because they weren't open to any of His answers.

Faith by the Sword?

In the silence of Jesus we see a respect for an individual's right to choose for or against Jesus—even at the cost of His life. This contrasts dramatically with what we see in others who claim to be from God. Let's look at three incredibly important areas.

Difference #1: In Christianity, conversion is your choice. Christian thinkers use the word *conversion* as a term for what happens in a person's life when he or she first trusts in Jesus. What conversion means is that every individual comes to know

God not because of family or culture or birthplace but only by a conscious choice to let Him have His rule in his or her life. Jesus' kingdom isn't of this world, and we don't enter His kingdom by physical birth.

We live in a time when angry voices demand that we shouldn't spread God's good news, that we shouldn't consider people "lost" just because they aren't Christians. Our "tolerant" culture says, "We are all born into different beliefs, and therefore, we should leave it that way." Mahatma Gandhi, for example, spoke out strongly against any sort of conversion.

People who argue this way forget or don't know that *nobody* is born a Christian. All Christians are Christians because they have been converted. Asking a Christian not to reach out to anyone from another faith is asking that Christian to deny his own faith.

> We live in a time when angry voices demand that we shouldn't consider people "lost" just because they aren't Christians.

One of India's leading "saints," Sri Ramakrishna, is said to have been for a little while a Muslim, for a little while a Christian, and then finally, a Hindu again, because he came to the conclusion that they are all the same. If that was true, why did he revert to Hinduism? As we have seen, it's just not true that all religions are the same. Even Hinduism isn't the same within itself. So to deny the Christian the privilege of sharing the Christian faith actually forces on him or her the beliefs of another religion.

Difference #2: In Christianity, compulsion is never an option. The teaching of Jesus is clear. No one should be compelled to become a Christian. On this point Christianity is drastically different from Islam.

In no country where Christianity is the faith of the majority is it illegal to spread another faith. There is no country in the world that I know of where renouncing the Christian faith puts a person in danger of being hunted down by the state. Yet there are many Islamic countries where it is against the law to publicly proclaim the good news of Jesus Christ, and where a Muslim who renounces his or her belief in Islam to follow any other faith risks death. Criticizing the Koran and Mohammed are prohibited by laws of blasphemy, and the result is torturous punishment. While we can respect the fact that a culture might want to protect what it says is important, forcing a belief in Jesus is foreign to the gospel. The contrast is crystal-clear.

God didn't intend the gospel to be spread at the point of a sword. When Christendom has resorted to methods of force, it wasn't the message of Jesus Christ that was spread but a political system that used the gospel as an excuse to wield power over institutions and individuals. People have reason to fear when they see religion married to political control. Jesus' method is to touch the heart of an individual so that he or she responds to Him out of love, rather than from being forced in any way to believe.

> There are many Islamic countries where it is against the law to publicly proclaim the good news of Jesus Christ.

The Sword of Mohammed

Compare this to the practice of Mohammed. However we might wish it away, the sword and warfare are basic parts of the Islamic faith. While some have resorted to force in the name of the Christian faith, *forcing someone to believe goes against the core of what we believe.* Do you see the difference?

How Can You Best Share What You Believe?

The silence of Jesus means that God gives people the spiritual freedom to say to you, "*I* don't want to hear any more." But it's never right when they say, "*You* can't say any more to *anyone else*" (Acts 5:27–29). God calls Christians to be ambassadors for Him, "as though God were making his appeal through us" (2 Cor. 5:20).

The whole Bible is your manual on how to be like Jesus as you explain Him to your world. But 1 Peter 3:15–16 is a passage filled with specific pointers: "But in your hearts set apart Christ as Lord. Always be prepared to give an answer to everyone who asks you to give the reason for the hope that you have. But do this with gentleness and respect, keeping a clear conscience, so that those who speak maliciously against your good behavior in Christ may be ashamed of their slander."

That passage raises some quick questions to ask yourself:

- "Christ as Lord"—Are you promoting Jesus or yourself?
- "Be prepared to give an answer"—Have you thought about *why* you believe?
- "For the hope"—What has Jesus accomplished for all people? And for you?
- "Gentleness and respect"—Are you aiming to *win an argument* or to *persuade a friend?*
- "Clear conscience"—Is there anything in your life that could cause people to rightly call you a hypocrite?

Even the best of apologists for Islam acknowledge the use of the sword in Islam, but they will soften the truth by saying that violence was used for defensive purposes. I suggest that you read the Koran and the history of Islam yourself to determine whether this is true.

As for executions, for example, that were carried out at Mohammed's command, his apologists argue that they weren't really ordered by him but just carried out on his behalf. Again, read for yourself to see if this defense matches the historic record.

Even the best of Muslim apologists is hard-pressed to skirt Mohammed's own injunction to kill found in a verse from the Koran known as the *ayatus-saif,* or "the verse of the sword":

> But when the forbidden months are past, then fight and slay the idolaters wherever ye find them, and take them, and prepare for them each ambush. But if they repent and establish worship and pay the poor due, then leave their way free. (Surah 9:5)

What one Islamic scholar says about the passage is also revealing:

> And a traitor guilty of high treason is an outlaw and may be killed by anyone without any special authority. May God guide us all to the Truth and spread peace and unity amongst mankind![2]

I shall say no more on this very difficult and divisive issue here because any comment would breed hard feelings, and that is not my desire. What it clearly boils down to is this: Where Islam and Christianity do agree is that truth is supreme; however, they see truth finally revealed in different persons—in Islam through Mohammed and in Christianity through Jesus Christ. This is why a comparison between the two persons is necessary.

Difference #3: In Christianity, the call of God is clear. The question the opponents of Jesus put to Him was this: *Aren't you going to answer us?* The Bible says, "The chief priests accused him of many things. So again Pilate asked him, 'Aren't you going to answer? See how many things they are accusing you of.' But Jesus still made no reply, and Pilate was amazed" (Mark 15:3–5).

> Jesus' silence doesn't mean He doesn't speak. He has already spoken in His Word, the Scriptures.

Jesus' silence doesn't mean He doesn't speak. He has already spoken in His Word, the Scriptures. In the Bible we find a unified, trustworthy message: Christ is the Savior of the world. He Himself is the final source of authority on what Christianity is all about.

This clarity of "revelation," the core message of a religion believed to have been communicated by God, is strikingly different from what we find in other faiths.

In Islam, there are questions about the perfection of the Koran. Muslims see the Koran, their scriptures, as the perfect and final revelation of Allah. The very words of the Koran are said to have been dictated by Allah to Mohammed, who is to the Muslim the last and the greatest prophet. The proof of Mohammed's supremacy is the perfection of the Koran.

It's hard, however, to maintain that the Koran is perfect. What about the grammatical flaws that have been demonstrated? Ali Dashti, an Iranian author and a committed Muslim, commented that the errors in the Koran were so many that the grammatical rules had to be altered in order to fit the claim that the Koran was flawless. He gives numerous examples of these in his book, *Twenty-Three Years: The Life of the Prophet Mohammed.* Dashti, by the way, allowed his book to be published only after his death.

In recent times, scholars have also begun to look at the Koran and have raised doubts about its origin and compilation. This has sent many Islamic scholars scrambling for a response.[3]

The poetry and the style of the Koran is indeed beautiful. But its demonstrated imperfections make it impossible to accept as God's Word.

In Hinduism, there is confusion about the meaning of Hindu scriptures. Hindus point to their scriptures as truth. The Hindu scriptures actually fall into two broad categories—the Smriti and the Sruti. *Smriti* means "that which is remembered." The authors are many, and the assertions they make are often polar opposites. In this body of writing lie speculations of Indian sages ranging from the profound to the utterly bizarre, by their own admission. *Sruti,* on the other hand, means "that which was revealed." This is the eternally true revelation of the devout Hindu, the basis of his or her faith.

This claim of eternally true revelation, however, raises huge questions. If "that which was revealed" is the eternal authority, then the obvious question for Hinduism, with its claim that all is One and we are all part of the Divine, is this: "Who is doing the revealing?" We can put it another way: Exactly who is telling us "truth"?

The implications of such a view of God and revelation knot our brains. If we all are God and yet we disagree, then which one of us is right about truth? If all beliefs contained in any one of our minds is either "God in ignorance" or "God in Enlightenment," which is which? When Buddha rejected the Hindu Scriptures, for example, was he God in ignorance or God in Enlightenment? When Mohammed said—contrary to Hindu scripture—that there is one God and his name is Allah, was he God in ignorance or God in Enlightenment? When all that exists is God, the questions collapse in on themselves. We can never be sure of what is true—or not.

In Christianity, there is a clear revelation of Christ. In Christianity, we receive a revelation that is entirely different. It is clear. It is unified. And it centers on Christ.

In chapter 4, we looked at some basic characteristics of Scripture. Now we can see how the utter reliability of our Bible provides a uniquely clear message.

- Remember, in contrast to Islam, the Bible does not have one author but many human authors writing over a fifteen-hundred-year span—writers from various backgrounds, times, and learning—who, under God's inspiration, wrote down the revelation.

- Over that vast span of time the biblical authors' message is one—they point to the birth, the death, and the resurrection of God's Son, Jesus Christ. That is an incredible agreement of thought over nearly two millennia, one that defies natural explanation. Long before everything intersected in the person of Jesus, His coming was envisioned, foreshadowed, described, and fulfilled. After His death, the written Scriptures spoke of Jesus' life, which was uniquely born, lived, crucified, and risen.

- And the climax of that Word is the person of Jesus Christ. The written Word is complete. He is perfect. He reminded us that the Scriptures can't be broken. In other words, God has spoken and given to us His Word.

This is a clarity of revelation unique among the faiths of the world.

God Is Never Silent

Even when Jesus stood quietly before Pilate, He was fulfilling Scripture. His silence before people who would take His life was predicted by the prophet Isaiah eight hundred years before it took place. "He was oppressed and afflicted, yet he did not open his mouth; he was led like a lamb to the slaughter, and as a sheep before her shearers is silent, so he did not open his mouth" (Isa. 53:7).

> To those of us who have ears willing to hear the truth, Jesus always speaks.

In a world of noise, the silence of God can be terrifying. Martin Luther once cried out, "Bless us Lord! Yea, even curse us. But please be not silent!" But God is never silent toward us. It's what the apostle Paul wrote to young Timothy:

> But as for you, continue in what you have learned . . . and how from infancy you have known the holy Scriptures, which are able to make you wise for salvation through faith in Christ Jesus. All Scripture is God-breathed and is useful for teaching, rebuking, correcting and training in righteousness, so that the man of God may be thoroughly equipped for every good work. (2 Tim. 3:14–17)

To those of us who have ears willing to hear the truth, Jesus always speaks.

SEVEN

WHO ARE YOU LOOKING FOR?

Many years ago, two philosophers told this parable to debunk God's existence:

> Once upon a time two explorers came upon a clearing in the jungle. In the clearing growing side by side were many flowers and many weeds. One of the explorers exclaimed, "Some gardener must tend this plot!" So they pitched their tents and set a watch.
>
> But though they waited several days no gardener was seen.
>
> "Perhaps he is an invisible gardener!" they thought. So they set up a barbed-wire fence and connected it to electricity. They even patrolled the garden with bloodhounds, for they remembered that H. G. Wells's "Invisible Man" could be both smelt and touched though he could not be seen. But no sounds ever suggested that someone had received an electric shock. No movements of the wire ever betrayed an invisible climber. The bloodhounds never alerted them to the presence of any other in the garden than themselves. Yet, still the believer between them was convinced that there was indeed a gardener.
>
> "There must be a gardener, invisible, intangible, insensible to electric shocks, a gardener who has no scent and makes no

sound, a gardener who comes secretly to look after the garden which he loves."

At last the skeptical explorer despaired. "But what remains of your original assertion? Just how does what you call an invisible, intangible, eternally elusive gardener differ from an imaginary gardener or even from no gardener at all?"[1]

How many times have we wished we could just see God so we could know for sure that He actually exists? We wait. We watch. But like the explorers looking for the gardener, we don't *see* Him—at least not quite in the way the skeptical explorer thought we should.

People who don't believe in God plead, "Show Him to me." Friends who follow other religions challenge, "Demonstrate to me that your God exists and that mine doesn't." And like the authors who wrote this parable, many ask, "What's the difference between an invisible, elusive gardener and no gardener at all?"

Is There a Gardener?

Is there a God? If there is, who is He? Christians believe that Jesus is the one true revelation of God and the one way to His home in heaven. But does that make our beliefs true?

So far we have seen the friends and foes of Jesus ask six questions to help them determine who He is. Jesus' answers are unique among the religions of the world—and, I believe, uniquely persuasive evidence that He alone is God.

To borrow an image from the garden parable, yes, there is a Gardener.

And yes, the Gardener is the God revealed fully in Jesus Christ.

In this chapter we bump into a question asked on Christ's behalf: "Who is it you are looking for?" (John 20:15). It's a question asked of Mary when she went to the garden where Jesus' body had been entombed.

During the few short years the disciples had been with Jesus, they had always been full of questions. They must have felt a small sting when this question was put to *them*. And this question echoed the toughest quizzes Jesus had given them as He discipled them. To His earliest followers, He had said, "What do you want?" (John 1:38). He had asked the disciples of John the Baptizer, "What did you go out into the desert to see?" (Matt. 11:7). Jesus repeatedly stopped His followers to make them realize exactly what it was they expected God to be to win their approval.

> Faith won't do you any good if the God you follow, worship, and commit your life to isn't real.

The angel asked, "Who is it you are looking for?" That is precisely the question of this book for you. What kind of God are you looking for? Are you searching for the One who is *real*? Remember? Faith won't do you any good if the God you follow, worship, and commit your life to isn't real.

You have to decide for yourself: Is Jesus genuine? Is He the one and only God?

Big Things Happen in Bible Gardens

The challenge at the beginning of this chapter was set in a garden. The atheists who chose that setting for their parable probably thought that a garden was a safe place to disprove God's existence. After all, no one has seen God in a garden, have they?

Why Not Hedge Our Bets?

Today's air of tolerance causes more and more people to buy into multiple spiritual traditions. *If one God is good,* people think, *then two must be better!* Let me explain why that isn't a workable faith.

- *Different religions truly point to different Gods.* The Koran, for example, claims Allah is the supreme being. The Bible says its God runs the universe. The moment you look at the claims of these two beings, you can't say they are the same. The Koran denies the resurrection, the very event that defines Christ and Christianity. The character of Allah and the biblical God differ drastically.

- *There is no such thing as two "equal" Gods.* If two Gods are different—and if by definition God is the One who has ultimate power and to whom we have ultimate accountability—both can't be ultimates. And if one is all-powerful and the other less powerful, then why have two?

- *If you have "another" God, then you don't have the biblical God.* God doesn't tolerate rivals. He calls us to an exclusive relationship. While this may sound egotistical, God is perfect and wants none of us to give our lives to anything less than His perfection.

If the world of religion is like a supermarket, you can only choose one God to take through the checkout line. A real God is too big to leave room in your cart for anything else.

Actually, we have. The story of Jesus, in fact, can be told around the setting of four gardens.

- In the garden of creation, we discover that Jesus is real.

- In the garden of temptation, we find that Jesus is righteous.

- In the garden of pain, we learn that Jesus is radical.

- In the garden of resurrection, we see that Jesus is risen.

I chose these gardens because they demonstrate one more time that Jesus is who He claims to be. They show that God is real. And they show who God is.

To put it in the terms of the parable once again, the Gardener exists. He is neither invisible nor elusive. He has spoken—not just in creation but face to face.

Because of Jesus we know the absolute truth of these facts.

Are you ready for the tour de gardens?

Snakes and Apples: The Garden of Creation

The Bible begins in a garden. Tragically, the Garden of Eden described in the first three chapters of Genesis is where many people's search for God starts and ends. Instead of looking at why that passage was written and what it actually says, atheists mock the biblical description of God's creation of the world as totally lacking in scientific sophistication. At the other extreme are Christians who read and defend the record of creation as if it were a doctoral dissertation in astrophysics.

In this struggle, both sides miss what Genesis is really about:

- *God is the Creator.* Genesis shows that God is both personal and eternal. He is a living God who communicates with His creation.

- *The world didn't come about by accident.* Our world is designed as a home for humanity and all the creatures of the world.

- *Life couldn't be lived alone.* The jewel of creation is man and woman, a pairing meant for relationship with God and each other.

- *Humans were made as moral entities.* God set human beings in place and entrusted the world to them. They have a choice in how they respond.

When we look at those all-important questions of why Genesis was written and what it actually says, these are some of the conclusions we can safely draw.

If you have ever had Genesis wrapped around your neck by an opponent of Christianity, however, you know that the debate doesn't end there. Here's the problem for the atheist: It takes enormous prejudice to thrust on Genesis our modern question of whether God created in six days or fifteen billion years. To answer that question wasn't the intention of Genesis at all, and no portion of Scripture ever claims to be a piece of scientific material intended to satisfy a twenty-first-century technician. I repeatedly hear critics ridicule the ancient belief that the earth was flat and that the world was created in 4004 B.C., beliefs they claim to be taught in the Bible. They never pause to prove their point by showing exactly where they find that in the Bible.

The debate, actually, is a lot like the Genesis story itself. You probably remember that into the perfect setting of the Garden of Eden entered Satan in the guise of a snake (Gen. 3:1). What you probably recall are the details of Adam and Eve and the apple. But the point of that story was that doubt was planted about whether God had really spoken and given the ground rules for life. Today those doubts surface again when people ask, "Did

God really say that?" Or "Did God really make that?" Or "Can we really look at the world and see any sign of God?" Or even "Is there really a Gardener?"

The Gardener isn't just in our imaginations. What we learn in the garden of creation is that God—Jesus—is *real*. We see evidence of Him in what He said and what He made, His handiwork all around us and even *in* us.

You might be wondering, by the way, what *Jesus* has to do with creation at the beginning of time. Understanding God as a Trinity—and Jesus as one person of that three-person being of Father, Son, and Holy Spirit—is a bigger discussion than we can enter into here. Yet remember that Jesus has been God from all eternity—and that the Bible specifically says, "For by him [Jesus] all things were created" (Col. 1:16).

Rocks and Hunger: The Garden of Temptation

The second garden lacks the lush foliage of the first. It's actually the desert where Jesus was tempted by Satan to chase a ministry different from what His Father intended (Matt. 4:1–11). The question in this setting wasn't whether God and His commands were real, but whether those commands could be twisted to mean something different—something that would better serve our purposes.

Jesus was hungry and physically weak, and the tempter stormed Him with a series of taunts: "Make bread—so You can eat." "Jump—and see if Your Father will honor His word." "Bypass the cross—and let me crown You king right now." Every temptation was infused with the same challenge: "Why don't You do this Your own way and prove You can run Your own life?"

Does that sound like a familiar lure you hear daily?

So how did Jesus respond? He said that He didn't live by bread alone but by God's words. He wouldn't put God to the test. And He would serve only God's purposes. When faced with an opportunity to rewrite God's will for His life, Jesus chose instead to do the right thing.

In contrast to Jesus, who refused to twist God's words or exalt Himself, we see other religions caving in to these temptations:

- Hinduism and Buddhism have repeatedly tried to shade the truths of our Scriptures to make them fit their own worldviews. Verses such as "The kingdom of God is within you" (Luke 17:21) or "I and the Father are one" (John 10:30) are said, for example, to support pantheism, the belief in many gods. (Reading the context of these verses, by the way, shows these interpretations convey anything but what the passages mean.)

- New Age spiritualities—belief systems rooted in Eastern religions—shuttle God off to the side and put self at the center. Rather than calling us to live according to God's commands, they allow us to shape a mysticism and morality of our own design. We can appeal to our spiritual bent and at the same time put ourselves center stage.

Hebrews 4:15 says Jesus was "tempted in every way, just as we are—yet was without sin." In the garden of temptation, we see that Jesus is *righteous* through and through.

Crosses and Choices: The Garden of Pain

What we see in the next garden are circumstances for which no other system even pretends to find a substitute. In this garden, Jesus kneels at the most desperate moment of His mission and makes a one-of-a-kind decision.

The Bible books of Matthew, Mark, Luke, and John all place Jesus at the Garden of Gethsemane when He was betrayed by His disciple Judas. Matthew gives us an extensive look at the anguish of Jesus in those moments preceding His arrest. He was lonely, sorrowful, and pained to the core as He thought about His impending death (Matt. 26:36–56).

But in the Garden of Gethsemane, Jesus cemented His choice to fulfill His mission, no matter what the cost. In Jesus' choice to follow God's plan, we see that Jesus was *radical*.

The radical nature of Christ's choice is even more stark in light of the ugliness of what Jesus chose to suffer on our behalf. In his extraordinary book *Crucifixion in the Ancient World and the Folly of the Cross,* Christian thinker Martin Hengel takes the reader through the grim historic details of crucifixion. Here are a few points Hengel makes about the meaning of Christ's death, things Jesus knowingly said yes to in order that He might save us:

> In the Garden of Gethsemane, Jesus cemented His choice to fulfill His mission, no matter what the cost.

- Crucifixion was a political and military punishment. The Romans who killed Jesus used it on the lowest classes of society—slaves, violent criminals, and the unruly.

- Crucifying an individual satisfied a lust for revenge and brought great sadistic pleasure. It was the triumph of the state.

- By displaying the victim naked at a prominent place, crucifixion represented the uttermost of humiliation.

- Often the victim's corpse was never buried so that wild beasts could feed on the carcass.[2]

Two thousand years later, we see the symbol of the cross on necklaces and on church steeples so often that we have no concept of what it meant. Try to both understand and feel these things:

- Those who hurt Jesus hated Him.

- Those who hated Him, Jesus loved.

- Those who killed Jesus wanted to be rid of Him.

- By allowing Himself to be killed, Jesus made it possible for them to live.

- By crucifying Jesus, humanity displayed the deepest possible rebellion against God.

This is what the radical choice of Jesus means: He came to lay down His life so that those who killed Him—people who were representatives of all of us—could be forgiven. Forgiveness is only possible because of the price that He paid in the hell of a world that does not recognize His voice.

A Rolled-Away Stone and a Risen Savior: The Garden of Resurrection

The Garden of Gethsemane immediately preceded Christ's death on the cross. But we have one more garden to examine.

After Jesus was crucified, two men came and asked Pilate for permission to take His body down from the cross and entomb Him. Both were afraid to follow Jesus openly when He was alive. One was Joseph of Arimathea, described by the Bible as a secret follower. The other was Nicodemus, a teacher who once had come secretly at night to visit Jesus to avoid being seen. Joseph and Nicodemus brought a sack of myrrh and aloes and strips of cloth to wrap Jesus' body in keeping with

Jewish custom. Having wrapped the body, they laid it in a tomb.

Even though Jesus was certifiably dead, Jesus' enemies were still nervous. They asked Pilate to post a guard around the tomb because they feared the body would be stolen by His disciples. The disciples could then claim that Jesus had risen from the dead on the third day just as He had pledged.

Amazing! Jesus' enemies evidently understood His promise to rise again from the dead better than His own followers did. His disciples were hiding in fear of being arrested and killed like Jesus. But His enemies took extra precautions to guard against the theft of Jesus' body.

The Bible says that before dawn on the first day of the week, Mary Magdalene went to that tomb and discovered the stone covering the tomb's entrance had been rolled away. She ran off to tell Simon Peter and John that the body of Jesus was missing—but "we don't know where they have put him" (John 20:2). Simon Peter and John ran to the tomb and confirmed that Jesus was gone, but they still didn't understand that He had risen from the dead (v. 9).

The story continues:

> Then the disciples went back to their homes, but Mary stood outside the tomb crying. As she wept, she bent over to look into the tomb and saw two angels in white, seated where Jesus' body had been. . . .
>
> They asked her, "Woman, why are you crying?"
>
> "They have taken my Lord away," she said, "and I don't know where they have put him." At this, she turned around and saw Jesus standing there, but she did not realize that it was Jesus.
>
> "Woman," he said, "why are you crying? Who is it you are looking for?"
>
> Thinking he was the gardener, she said, "Sir, if you have carried him away, tell me where you have put him, and I will get him."
>
> Jesus said to her, "Mary." (vv. 10–16)

When Jesus had spoken and said, "I am the way and the truth and the life" (John 14:6), He claimed what no other did. When He had said, "My sheep listen to my voice; I know them, and they follow me. I give them eternal life, and they shall never perish; no one can snatch them out of my hand" (John 10:27–28), He spoke as no other did. And now, risen from the dead, He had done what no other has ever accomplished.

In the second chapter of Philippians, the Bible has a riveting summary of Jesus' walk through the garden of pain and the garden of resurrection.

> . . . Being in very nature God, [Jesus] did not consider equality with God something to be grasped, but made Himself nothing, taking the very nature of a servant, being made in human likeness. And being found in appearance as a man, he humbled himself and became obedient to death—even death on a cross! Therefore God exalted him to the highest place and gave him the name that is above every name, that at the name of Jesus every knee should bow, in heaven and on earth and under the earth, and every tongue confess that Jesus Christ is Lord, to the glory of God the Father. (vv. 6–11)

Jesus is not dead. He is Real. Righteous. Radical. Risen.

This is the Jesus who called Mary by name and asked her, "Why are you crying? Who are you looking for?"

When Mary came looking for the body of Jesus, she discovered the most startling truth of all. The man she mistook for the gardener was Jesus. He was *risen*. And *He had come looking for her.*

Jesus is not dead. He is
   Real.
         Righteous.
            Radical.
               Risen.

Yes, There Is a Gardener

When the Christian thinker John Frame read the parable that starts this chapter, he responded with a brilliant counterargument. This is his parable:

> Once upon a time, two explorers came upon a clearing in the jungle. A man was there, pulling weeds, applying fertilizer, trimming branches. The man turned to the explorers and introduced himself as the royal gardener. One explorer shook his hand and exchanged pleasantries. The other ignored the gardener and turned away.
>
> "There can be no gardener in this part of the jungle," he said. "This must be some trick. Someone is trying to discredit our secret findings."
>
> They pitched camp. And every day the gardener arrived to tend the garden. Soon it was bursting with perfectly arranged blooms. But the skeptical explorer insisted, "He's only doing it because we are here—to fool us into thinking that this is a royal garden."
>
> One day the gardener took them to the royal palace and introduced the explorers to a score of officials who verified the gardener's status. Then the skeptic tried a last resort, "Our senses are deceiving us. There is no gardener, no blooms, no palace, no officials. It's all a hoax!"
>
> Finally the believing explorer despaired, "But what remains of your original assertion? Just how does this mirage differ from a real gardener?"[3]

There is so much evidence for the gardener, John Frame is saying, that only willful prejudice tries to explain it away.

Deciding for the Real Jesus—or Not

Your peers are testing truth, trying to decide if Jesus—or Buddha or Krishna or Mohammed—is real. Some are honest questioners. But others are dishonest skeptics, driven by willful prejudice.

The danger of your friends—Christian or not—easing Jesus out of their lives is entirely real.

Check out this well-known case. A man named Edmund Gosse once wrote a powerful book called *Father and Son*. It's the gripping true account of a son's struggle between the faith of his father and his own growing doubts of God's existence. His father was a marine biologist while he, the son, was a literature professor who later became the librarian at the British House of Lords. In the book, he traced his journey into skepticism to the day when he finally told his father that he was through with God and could no longer believe in His existence.

The father wrote back in gut-wrenching terms. Toward the end of the book, Gosse quotes that whole letter and says, "It buried itself like an arrow within my heart." Here are some pieces from his father's letter:

My dear Son,
    When your mother died, she not only tenderly committed you to God, but left you as a solemn charge to me, to bring you up in the nurture and admonition of the Lord. That responsibility I have sought to keep before me. . . . Before your childhood passed, there seemed God's manifest blessing on your care; for you seemed truly converted to Him. . . . All this filled my heart with thankfulness and joy. . . .

[But] when you came to us in the summer, the heavy blow fell upon me; and I discovered how very far you had departed from God. It was not that you had yielded to the strong tide of youthful blood . . . it was that which had already worked in your mind . . . sapping the very foundations of faith. . . . Nothing seemed left to which I could appeal. We had, I found, no common ground. The Holy Scriptures had no longer any authority. . . . Any oracle of God which pressed you, you could easily explain away; even the very character of God you weighed in your balance of reason and fashioned it accordingly. You were thus sailing down the rapid tide towards eternity without a single authoritative guide (having cast your chart overboard), except what you might fashion and forge on your own anvil. . . .

It is with pain, not in anger that I [write] . . . hoping that you may be induced to review the whole course, of which this is only a stage, before God. If this grace were granted to you, oh! How joyfully should I bury all the past, and again have sweet and tender fellowship with my beloved son, as of old.[4]

That is how the letter ended. Edmund made his response, telling the reader that he had a choice either "to retain his intelligence and reject God" or "to reject his intelligence and submit to God." This is how he closed his book, speaking in the third person:

And thus desperately challenged, the young man's conscience threw off once and for all the yoke of his "dedication," and as respectfully as he could, without parade or remonstrance, he took a human being's privilege to fashion his inner life for himself.[5]

The relationship between father and son was permanently severed.

How did all this happen? When young Gosse read Charles

Darwin's *Origin of Species,* in which Darwin issued what became the greatest challenge to God's existence in the modern world, he concluded that he was willing to forfeit everything to strike out on his own. If God didn't exist, he would run his own life.

Reasons to Believe

Gosse imagined that by rejecting God he was hanging on to his intelligence. Others who reject Christianity think that they are pursuing a higher level of tolerance. We are pummeled with the message that the smartest and kindest people in this world don't believe in the God of the Bible.

We need to be able to calmly critique other belief systems. We need to be able to match wits with people who think we are witless. But it's more important to consistently call to mind this fact: What we find in Jesus is unequaled reality. He offers us powerful reasons to believe:

- The claims of Jesus are uniquely *credible.* Jesus' unique, exclusive declarations are supported by evidence offered by no other faith, from the miracle of His birth to His absolute purity to His earthshaking resurrection.

- The claims of Jesus are uniquely *defensible.* The claims of Jesus have withstood two thousand years of objections.

- The claims of Jesus are uniquely *consistent.* The reality of who Jesus is can be observed not just in His teachings but in His entire life.

In a world of many gods, Jesus is absolute truth. He is beyond comparison. He is real, righteous, radical, and risen. We can't settle for anything less.

While your friends and peers may dabble in all sorts of alternative religions and even atheism, you can be sure of what you believe. Unsuspecting people make a fatal mistake when they pledge allegiance to a belief system for a few good points while ignoring its many contradictions. They might connect with some unique, attractive features of a faith—but they also unintentionally buy into untrue teachings or an unworthy leader.

In Jesus—and Jesus alone—we get God.

Is This for You?

The evidence demonstrates that we have incredible reasons to believe in Jesus and His uniqueness.

The evidence is abundant.

What we might lack is the willingness to deal with the evidence and its consequences for life.

Once we are persuaded by the evidence, however, only one thing remains: to respond in trust to the God who has shown Himself to us.

When missionary John Paton arrived in the South Pacific islands of the New Hebrides in the mid-1800s, he began translating the New Testament. He first had to give the native language an alphabet and put the language in writing. He worked with a young helper to come up with the vocabulary.

Paton struggled most with how to illustrate the word *believe*. One day, though, when he leaned completely on a chair in such a way that his whole weight was on it, he came up with the concept of trust. In their Bible, John 3:16 now reads, "For God so loved the world, that He gave His one and only Son, that whoever throws his whole weight on Him, will not perish but have eternal life."

May you throw the whole weight of your life on the One who is absolutely true.

NOTES

Chapter 2: Where Do You Live?

1. Used by personal permission of Larry King.

Chapter 3: How Do We Know the Claims of Jesus Are True?

1. Bertrand Russell, "An Outline of Intellectual Rubbish" (1950), as cited in *Columbia Dictionary of Quotations* (New York: Columbia University Press, 1993), http://www.geocities.com/Athens/Delphi/2795/outline_of_intellectual_rubbish.

2. Thomas Nagel, *The Last Word* (New York: Oxford University Press, 1997), 130.

3. David Hume, *On Human Nature and the Understanding*, ed. Anthony Flew (New York: Collier Books, 1962), 163.

Chapter 4: Won't Jesus Make Life Wonderful?

1. Norman Geisler, "How Can We Know the Bible Is the Word of God?" in *The Compact Guide to World*

Religions, ed. Dean C. Halverson (Minneapolis: Bethany House Publishers, 1996), 257.

2. Jon Krakauer, *Into Thin Air* (New York: Villard Books, 1996), 187–88.

3. David A. Brown, *A Guide to Religions* (London: SPCK, 1975), 148.

4. Deepak Chopra, *The Seven Spiritual Laws of Success* (San Rafael, Calif.: Amber Allen Publishing, 1994), 68–69.

5. Ibid., 98.

6. Ibid., 102.

7. See Radhakrishnan in his *Hindu View of Life* (New Delhi, India: Indus, 1993), and Pandit Nehru in his comment on Hinduism, quoted in Brown, *A Guide to Religions*, 63.

Chapter 5: Is God Responsible For My Pain?

1. Richard Dawkins, *Out of Eden* (New York: Basic Books, 1992), 133.

2. Richard Dawkins, "Viruses of the Mind," *1992 Voltaire Lecture* (London: British Humanist Association, 1993), 9.

3. Elie Wiesel, quoted in Dennis Ngien, "The God Who Suffers," *Christianity Today*, 3 February 1997, 40.

Chapter 6: Won't Jesus Answer Every Question?

1. Quoted in Harry Paddon Liddon, *Liddon's Bampton Lectures 1866* (London: Rivingtons, 1869), 148.

2. Hafiz Ghulam Sarwar, *Muhammad: The Holy Prophet* (Lahore, Pakistan: Sh. Muhammad Ashraf, 1969), 195.

3. For those interested in following up on the most recent challenges, I recommend reading the January 1999 issue of *Atlantic Monthly*, which contains a fascinating article on Koranic studies: "What Is the Koran," by Toby Lester, 43–56.

Chapter 7: Who Are You Looking For?

1. Anthony Flew, "Theology and Falsification," in John Hick, ed., *The Existence of God* (New York: Collier Books, 1964), 225.

2. Martin Hengel, *Crucifixion in the Ancient World and the Folly of the Cross* (Philadelphia: Fortress Press, 1977), 86–88.

3. John Frame, "God and Biblical Language: Transcendence and Immanence" in J. W. Montgomery (Ed.), *God's Inerrant Word* (Minneapolis: Bethany Fellowship), 171.

4. Edmund Gosse, *Father and Son* (New York: Penguin Books, 1907, 1989), 249–51.

5. Ibid., 16–17.

ALSO AVAILABLE FROM RAVI ZACHARIAS

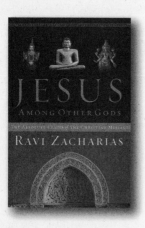

Jesus Among Other Gods

In a world with so many religions—why Jesus? In his most important work to date, apologetics scholar and popular speaker Ravi Zacharias shows how the blueprint for life and death is found in a true understanding of Jesus. *Jesus Among Other Gods* contrasts the truth of Jesus with founders of Islam, Hinduism, and Buddhism, strengthening believers and compelling them to share their faith with our postmodern world.

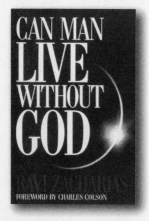

Can Man Live Without God

In this brilliant apologetic defense of the Christian faith—the likes of which we haven't seen since C. S. Lewis—Ravi Zacharias exposes the emptiness of life without God, discussing subjects including antitheism, the meaning of life, and the person of Jesus.

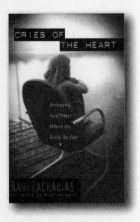

Cries of the Heart

One of the greatest thinkers of our time covers new ground by exploring the deepest cries of the human heart. Through moving stories and relevant questions, Ravi Zacharias invites readers to join him in finding answers to the question: How can things be right when they feel so wrong?

Deliver Us from Evil

In this compelling volume, Ravi Zacharias examines the mystery of evil. This brilliant writer and gifted teacher traces how secularization has led to a loss of shame, pluralization has led to a loss of reason, and privatization has led to a loss of meaning in today's culture.

About the Author

Ravi Zacharias is president of Ravi Zacharias International Ministeries. Born in India, he has lectured in more than fifty countries and in several of the world's most prominent universities. He is the author of numerous books, including *Can Man Live Without God, Deliver Us from Evil,* and *Cries of the Heart.* His weekly radio program "Let My People Think" is heard on numerous radio stations across the country. He and his wife, Margie, are the parents of three children.

Kevin Johnson is the bestselling author of almost twenty youth books. Former pastor of more than four hundred youth at Elmbrook Church in metro Milwaukee, he holds an M.Div. from Fuller Theological Seminary and a B.A. in English and journalism from the University of Wisconsin. Kevin is a full-time author and speaker and lives in Minnesota with his wife, Lyn, and their three children.

For more information about Kevin's books, visit his web site at
www.thewave.org.